Seeing and Feeling the Church

— *Expanded Edition* —

Bill Freeman

Ministry Publications
Scottsdale, Arizona

Expanded Edition 1997

ISBN 0-914271-39-3

Library of Congress
Catalog Number: 96-76219

Ministry Publications
P.O. Box 12222
Scottsdale, Arizona 85267
(602) 948-4050 / Fax (602) 922-1338
E-mail: MinWord12@aol.com

Printed in the United States of America

Contents

1 ▶ Paul's Prayer to *See* the Church
(Ephesians 1:16-23)

To summarize the apostle Paul's burden for all believers is quite simple. It is opened up in the two prayers found in the book of Ephesians. Both of these prayers specifically relate to the two major things that we as believers need — to see the church and to feel the church. Let us look at the burden that is expressed in these two prayers. The first prayer is in Ephesians 1. It is a prayer for all the saints to *see* the church — to have a spirit of wisdom and revelation, with the eyes of their heart enlightened to see what is the highest thing in this universe. This is to see the church as it is described by Paul in his prayer in chapter 1.

Thus, the first prayer is a prayer for sight, for revelation. It is a prayer for our experience after we are saved, after we find the Lord and are regenerated. We are born again and we love the Lord, we love the saints, and we love the Bible. We are growing in the Lord, and we realize something has inwardly happened to us. Now there is a specific prayer for you and for me as believers. This prayer is that we would have a spirit of wisdom and revelation in the full knowledge of God. It is a prayer to *see* something — to have our minds renewed by the unveiling of the Word of God concerning God's heart's desire.

God's desire is focused in His masterpiece, the church. Ephesians 2:10 says, "We are His workmanship" (KJV). This word "workmanship" comes from the Greek word *poiema* (ποίημα) and can be translated "masterpiece" or "poem." It refers to someone's best work. As God's chosen and redeemed people, we are His best work in this universe. We are His masterpiece, created in Christ Jesus. Praise the Lord! We are ones to be conformed to Him as the many brothers of Christ (Rom. 8:29), as the many members of His Body (1 Cor. 12:12-13, 27), and as the living stones of the house of God (1 Pet. 2:5).

The church is God's heart's desire. It is higher than our individual spirituality and higher than any "victorious life" in an individualistic way. As good as these may be, there is something higher. What is higher is the corporate habitation of God in the spirits of His people, where He has real freedom and access not only to live, but to move and have His expression. To express His fullness requires the whole Body; no one individual contains the fullness. The fullness is in all the members. Thus, the church, which is His Body, is the fullness of Him, the One who is presently filling all in all (Eph. 1:22-23). We need to see the church according to this divine revelation.

Again, the prayer and the burden in Ephesians 1 is a prayer for revelation. It is a prayer for sight. It means that one day the full knowledge of God must be opened up to us. Let us look at Ephesians 1:17-18a: [17] "That the God of our Lord Jesus Christ, the Father of glory, may give to you a spirit of wisdom and revelation in the full knowledge of Him, [18a] the eyes of your heart being enlightened." In other words, to receive a spirit of wisdom and revelation requires the full knowledge of God to be opened up to us from the apostles' New Testament ministry.

At this point it is important to consider how God created man. As human beings we are made up of three parts: our spirit, soul, and body (1 Thess. 5:23). Our soul also includes three parts: our mind, emotions, and will. The deepest part of our being is our spirit, created by God for Christ to actually live inside of us. Christ is not merely a thought in our mind, nor is He merely a feeling in our emotion. Christ is a person, resurrected and alive and located within our spirit. When we received Christ, our spirit was regenerated, born of God. We were made alive to God. Now our spirit is joined to the Lord (1 Cor. 6:17). We are organically joined to Another life.

Our mind needs the proper understanding of the full knowledge of God so that our spirit will also be proper. Our spirit needs to be fed with the right food. It needs the spirit-food of the Word with the apostles' revelation and vision of the full knowledge of God. We need to see what they saw, to feel what they felt, to touch God's heart the way they touched God's heart. We need to enter into the apostles' understanding concerning God's heart's desire in the universe.

We actually enter into the apostles' vision and revelation. We are not making up something new. We are not fabricating something. We are believers who are entering into the *identical revelation* that Paul, Peter, and John had (Eph. 3:2-4; 2 Pet. 3:2; 2 John 8). So Paul prays that the believers would have a spirit of wisdom and revelation in the sphere of the full knowledge of God. This is a prayer for sight and revelation to see the church.

Many of us could give testimonies about seeing the church. I myself was saved for years. I was regenerated and I was filled with the Holy Spirit, possessing the gifts of the Spirit, bringing people to the Lord — having all these kinds of experiences. Yet I was deficient in my sight concerning the church. I didn't see the church. You say, "What do you mean you didn't see the church? Just look down the street—there's the Baptist church and there's the Methodist church." This is often people's concept, that the church is a physical building. But to understand the church in this way is too low. The church is God's chosen and redeemed people indwelt by Him. This is what He desires.

THE THREE "WHATS" OF PAUL'S PRAYER

We need to have revelation concerning the church. We need to see it. I saw the church by hearing a ministry that opened up the full knowledge of God. I didn't fully know why I was a believer. I didn't know the three "whats" of Paul's prayer in Ephesians chapter 1. I didn't have any understanding of the purpose of those "whats." In Ephesians 1:18 Paul says, "The eyes of your heart being enlightened, that you may know *what* is the hope of His calling." This is the first what. Then Paul continues, "and *what* are the riches of the glory of His inheritance in the saints." This is the second what. And finally in verse

19 he says, "and **what** is the exceeding greatness of His power toward us who believe, according to the operation of the might of His strength." This is the third what. So by looking at this prayer, we see that it is a prayer for a spirit of wisdom and revelation in the full knowledge of God. This full knowledge includes the three "whats" from verses 18 to 23.

The hope of His calling in eternity past

Now let us look more closely at the three "whats." First, **what** is the hope of His calling? "His calling" refers back to what happened over us before the foundation of the world — we were chosen in Him. Second Timothy 1:9 says, "[God] who has saved us, and called us with a holy calling, not according to our works, but according to His own purpose and grace, which was given to us in Christ Jesus *before time began.*" We were saved and then we were called with a holy calling. This holy calling is according to His purpose.

With His purpose, there is the endowment to carry it out. This endowment is grace. For example, you might have a purpose — to manufacture an automobile. You have created it in your thought.

You have designed it. You know exactly the way it is supposed to be. But you must have money to produce it. In other words, you can have purpose, but you need the means to execute it. God gave us purpose. The purpose is that we would be saturated with Himself in order that He would have a corporate expression (Eph. 1:4-5; Rom. 8:29). With this purpose He gave the grace (Eph. 1:6). The grace is the riches — the money. God gives us the spiritual riches of His grace to carry out His purpose. Brothers and sisters, we are all objects of the grace of God and partakers of His grace. He took us out of the world, out of vanity, and He put us into Himself to enjoy the riches of His grace (Eph. 1:7). Now He is doing a work in us to transform us to live according to His one unique purpose.

There is such hope rising up within me day by day because I know what His calling is over my life. I know that my destiny is Christ and the church. This was all decided before the foundation of the world. I know that everything that happens in my life — all the good and all the bad, all the environments, all the circumstances — everything is for me once again to travel the pathway of my spirit to enjoy my Christ and to experience His all-sufficiency within. So I have need of nothing. I know how to abound, and I know how to be abased (Phil. 4:12). I know how to pass through good environments, and I know how to pass through bad environments. Paul says it clearly: "For to me, to live is Christ" (Phil. 1:21). What does it profit you if you have something good? It is all vanity. What matters is Christ. This is the hope of God's calling.

Do you know that from eternity past God has had a design over you? It is not *your* plan. It is not your purpose, or mine, or anyone else's. It is God's. And this purpose is that you would be a person who is experiencing Christ and being saturated with Him for God's masterpiece — His building, the church. God purposed that you would be a living stone built up with other stones corporately for His house.

Paul's prayer is for sight, that is, for the full knowledge of God. As we hear the full knowledge, it is a marvelous thing if you and I have an inner "Amen," a response that can echo what we have heard. In Luke 7:32 the Lord exposed the improper responses within man: "We have played the flute for you, and *you did not dance;* we have sung a dirge, and *you did not weep.*" In other words, we talk and speak about these things, and we are waiting —

whose spirit will respond? Who will hear it? Brothers and sisters, may the Lord find in us a responsive spirit that can become a spirit of wisdom and revelation as the full knowledge of God is opened up to us through the ministry of His Word.

The riches of the glory of
His inheritance in eternity future

In Ephesians 1:18b Paul speaks of the second what: "***what*** are the riches of the glory of His inheritance in the saints." Again, God's calling over us is from eternity past. Paul wants us to know what is God's purpose in eternity past, and then what are the riches of the glory of His inheritance in the saints. His inheritance refers to eternity future. God has an inheritance in the saints! It is an awesome thought to realize that we are the objects of God's grace because we have been chosen by Him to be His inheritance. He is inheriting us, and we are inheriting Him. Thus, in eternity future our God has an eternal dwelling place, a habitation that He has inherited. What has He inherited? He has inherited an enlargement of His firstborn Son, the Christ, the One who has come into all of us and made us organically His Body (1 Cor.

12:12). And now God is inheriting this enlarged Christ for eternity. To know "what are the riches of the glory of His inheritance in the saints" is related to eternity future and is part of the full knowledge.

Paul prays that we as believers would have a spirit of wisdom and revelation to know where we came from, what we are doing here, and where we are going. These three questions should be answered by every human being. Do you know where you came from? Do you know what you are doing here? Do you know where you are going? We must answer these questions not from our own ideas or philosophy, but directly from God's revelation. We came from God's calling in eternity past, and we are destined to be His inheritance in eternity future. Now let us look at what we are doing here between these two ends of eternity.

The description of His power
to carry out His purpose in time

The third ***what*** is in verse 19: "And ***what*** is the exceeding greatness of His power toward us who believe, according to the operation of the might of His strength." Now Paul wants us to know what is the greatness of God's power. This power is embodied in resurrection life. Thus, it is resurrection power. Concerning this power, Paul says in Ephesians 1:20-23, [20] "Which He [God] caused to operate in Christ in raising Him from the dead and seating Him at His right hand in the heavenlies, [21] far above all rule and authority and power and lordship and every name that is named not only in this age but also in that which is to come; [22] and He subjected all things under His feet and gave Him to be Head over all things to the church, [23] which is His Body, the fullness of the One who fills all in all." This means that God operated and vested all that power in Christ, not for Him merely to be a Savior of individuals, but for Him to be Head over all things to the church.

God wants us to know that the power that raised Christ from the dead is the power to carry out *what* He planned in eternity past with His calling. He also wants us to know *what* He will obtain by this same power in eternity future with His inheritance. And now, in time, He wants us to know *what* is the surpassing greatness of His power that has been installed directly into our spirit. The power of this resurrected Christ indwells us *to do everything* in order to accomplish God's purpose of transforming our soul and saturating our body. By this power we become persons who are conformed to His image and organically connected to all the members of His Body. His exceedingly great power is now carrying out this purpose. This is Paul's prayer in Ephesians 1. It is a prayer for revelation. It is a prayer to have sight concerning our Christian life. Without this sight we are just drifting and living aimlessly. We must know specifically what God's calling is, what His inheritance is, and what His present power is.

This power is now working in us. It has already operated in us to regenerate our spirit. And in the remaining chapters of the book of Ephesians, we see a dynamic working-out of God's power in us. Ephesians 2 shows that we were once persons walking according to the age of this world, under the devil, conducting ourselves in the lusts of our flesh, with the sinful and fleshly drives that controlled us (vv. 1-3). Then by grace God made us alive together with Christ (v. 5). His power came into us and did something over our spirit. He made us alive through regeneration. And then in chapters 3 through 6 we see the power operating to produce what God planned in eternity past for eternity future — the church.

2 ▶ Paul's Prayer to *Feel* the Church
(Ephesians 3:14-21)

Following Paul's prayer in Ephesians 1, he prays another prayer in chapter 3. This prayer is for the believers to experience something further after they have seen the church by revelation. Our spirit may be a spirit of wisdom and revelation. We may be able to see God's eternal purpose. We may even be able to share with others about eternity past and eternity future and how God is now working out His plan for the church. This seeing is one thing, but Paul has a second prayer. This prayer is not merely a prayer to *see* the church, but a prayer to *feel* the church. Paul is praying for a deeper and further realization.

Perhaps a number of us could say there has been some answer to that first prayer in our realization — we have seen the church. But probably fewer of us could really correspond to the second prayer by saying, "I not only *see* the church, I *feel* the church. The church is in my desires, it is in my care, it is in my heart, it is in my concern, it is in my thoughts, it is in my anxieties, it is in my laboring, it is in my daily life, it is in my prayers, it is in my blood." This is to feel the church. We may be able to declare in the meetings, "I have seen the church!" But in our experience we may be very deficient in having a heart that feels and cares for the practical church life. This is why Paul prayed a second prayer. In Ephesians 1—3 he is burdened for sight and revelation concerning the church, but in Ephesians 4—6 he is burdened for the heart and the care to live out the practical church life. Thus, immediately before he opens up the details of the practical church life in chapter 4, he prays a second prayer for the believers at the end of chapter 3. This prayer is for a subjective experience of Christ to make home in our hearts so that we would have a capacity to care for and feel the church life.

The difference between
seeing and feeling the church

In Ephesians 3:14-15 Paul prays, [14] "For this cause I bow my knees to the Father, [15] of whom every family in the heavens and on earth is named." The "cause" that Paul is praying for here is the cause of *God's building* revealed in chapter 2, which is *the church* as God's eternal purpose in chapter 3, verses

10-11. After he mentions "the eternal purpose which He [God] purposed in Christ Jesus," then he begins to pray based upon "this cause." Thus, Paul's prayer is fully based upon the vision of God's eternal purpose to have the church as His building.

Paul says in verses 16-19, [16] "That He [the Father] would grant you, according to the riches of His glory, to be strengthened with power through His Spirit into the inner man, [17] that Christ may *make His home* in your hearts through faith, that you, being rooted and grounded in love, [18] may be able to apprehend with all the saints what the breadth and length and height and depth are [19] and to know the knowledge-surpassing love of Christ, that you may be filled unto all the fullness of God." "Apprehend" is a word that means to experience something, to lay hold of something. It means to actually feel it, to know it subjectively, experientially. This refers to something different from mere knowledge. We may know something about the church, but to apprehend and practically experience it touches our inner being so that we feel it. It is an apprehending that is living within our soul and heart.

This prayer is for a deeper experience in our relationship with the church. Here our realization of the church moves from the realm of revelation and sight to the realm of experience where our heart and feelings are involved. The first prayer is a prayer for revelation and aims at our spirit. The second prayer is a prayer for experience and aims at our heart and soul. Our apprehending and feeling are matters of the heart and soul.

When we receive the Lord, He comes into our spirit. But His goal is to use our spirit as a beachhead to possess our entire being. This is similar to soldiers landing on an ocean shore to establish a beachhead for the purpose of taking over a whole island. Our spirit is like a beachhead where the Lord has come into us. Now His purpose is to gradually take us over until He settles down and makes home in our heart. As He makes home in our heart, we begin to have feelings for the church in our heart. We are rooted and grounded in love, and we begin to love and care for the church in the same way He loves and cares for the church. Thus, we can say that we "feel the church" in our heart and soul.

Feeling responsible for the church in our hearts

Paul's prayer in Ephesians 3:16 is that we would

be strengthened into our inner man, that is, into our spirit as our source. Why? Because there is no other source or realm that has the power to change our hearts and souls. In verse 17 we see the result of this strengthening: "That Christ may make His home in your hearts through faith" — really settle down in you. It is not that He is just visiting your heart. He is making His home there. For Christ to make His home there is for Christ to feel through you, for Christ to react through you, for Christ to care through you.

If our heart and affections are occupied with other things, or if our heart has another goal or motive besides God's goal, then we will be a brother or sister who may have seen the church, but who cannot feel the church in our heart. Neither will we be able to have a genuine care for the church. Nor will we have the kind of responses that indicate that we regard the church as our own responsibility. But when the Lord gains our heart and affections, the church becomes to us a matter of personal responsibility. The church is *our* house! The church is *our* family! We care for the church not out of duty, but because we are constrained by a sense of personal burden. To us the meetings are not in the realm of mere nominal church attendance. Neither is our giving a token matter. To give a tithe or offering can be merely a religious routine without any deep sentiment for the church. However, when we feel the church, we realize our money belongs wholly to the Lord. Whatever He speaks to us, we will give. We have desires to give all when we have a heart for the church.

Let me share a practical example of what it means to feel the church. There were weeds growing up in front of the building where we meet. Though I was very busy, I was bothered by the poor testimony of having those weeds standing there. I was going to ask if someone would have time to cut them down, but I never made the connection with anyone. Then a few mornings later I noticed that one of our brothers and two of his children were cutting down all the weeds. I went out and said to the brother, "Who asked you to do this?" He replied, "I just saw that the weeds were getting too high, and I did it." The impression I received from him was that *he felt* the church's meeting place was his own responsibility. This brother's action is a good example of having a proper feeling for the church.

The things of the church should be carried upon all our hearts. First Corinthians 14:33 reflects this attitude: "For God is not a God of confusion but of peace, as in all the churches of the saints." To identify the churches as "the churches of the saints" indicates that the churches *belonged to* the saints. The churches are, as it were, the personal property and responsibility of the saints. In other words, the church is not something detached from us. It is not a mere objective thing that we go to or give to. Neither is it something that we "check out," so to speak, to see whether or not we like it. That is surely not seeing or feeling the church. The church is *us* in a subjective way.

When Paul describes the church in Ephesians 5:28-30 he says, [28b] "He who loves his wife loves himself. [29] For no one ever hated his own flesh, but nourishes and cherishes it, even as Christ also the church, [30] because we are members of His Body." Thus, the church is not only something we see by revelation, but it is something we apprehend and feel in our experience. When Christ loves the church, He is loving Himself, because the church is *His* Body. Similarly, when Christ loves the church *in* us and *through* us, we sense that we also love the church as ourselves, for we are members one of another (Rom. 12:5).

In Ephesians 3:17 when Paul says, "that Christ may make His home in your hearts through faith," he is speaking in the context of the church. The result of Christ making home in *our* hearts (plural) is that there is an ability infused into us by the power of the Spirit. This ability is to apprehend *with all the saints* the vast dimensions of the knowledge-surpassing love of Christ (vv. 18-19). This is a corporate feeling of love and a corporate sense of responsibility about the church. It is similar to how we feel about our own home. If something breaks or wears out, we take care of it. If the grass gets too high, we feel responsible to see that it gets cut. Why? Because it is *our* home. So we take care of it. If we have normal feelings, we will naturally manage and care for our own properties and belongings.

When we have the feeling of care for the church, it will express itself in many practical ways — from burdens to pray, to burdens to give, to feeling responsible to serve the saints in practical ways, to making many kinds of sacrifices — all of which demonstrate that the church is not something separate from us. The church is both God's home (1 Tim. 3:15) and our home. His home is our home. The church is a mutual abode to God and man (John 14:2).

The church is not an impersonal place. The church should not be a place where the pastor attempts to motivate people to be more committed, as though the congregation were doing God a favor to give their time and money to the church. Many of us could testify that this was our experience in the past. However, when you see the church by revelation and when you experience Christ at a deeper level — where He actually makes home in your heart — you *feel* the church. You find within you a genuine care for the Body of Christ.

Being dealt with in our motives

You cannot just work up these caring feelings. Unless you and I have a heart that has been purified from every motive other than God Himself, we are going to be people who may *see* something of the church, but cannot genuinely *feel* the church with our heart. Our consecration will be minimal. Our ability to give ourselves will be minimal. Consecration and givingness does not happen by mere instant inspiration at a revival meeting. Consecration is a solid and steady response to the revelation we have of the church.

When our revelation is high, like Paul's in the book of Ephesians, we see what God's good pleasure is in this universe. Our automatic response to this revelation is to pour ourselves out to the Lord. That is why Paul speaks in Romans 12 of presenting our bodies a living sacrifice. He does not merely coax and plead with people to give themselves to the Lord. His speaking is based upon eleven chapters of revelation preceding chapter 12. He opens up the corporateness of God's people, and then he says, "I exhort you *therefore,* brothers, through the compassions of God, that you present your bodies a living sacrifice" (12:1). You are here as a member because of His mercy, His compassions. He chose you before the foundation of the world, with His calling and for His inheritance. He is now working out this purpose. Therefore, you can present your body a living sacrifice.

We must realize we are persons giving ourselves to the Lord based upon revelation. You may have had revelation, but you may lack the freshness of it because of a deficiency in your experience of Christ making home in your heart. That is why we need to experience the Lord in the context of Paul's ministry — the church life. In the church life we experience that the Lord not only regenerates us in our spirit but He also begins to spread in us, possessing our heart and soul.

The glory in the church is not only in having our

spirits released, but also in having the Spirit pass through our purified souls and hearts. It is in the heart and in the soul that the glory of God is ultimately expressed.   When Christ is lived out, there is a pureness and a precious glory that is on the surface of our being. You feel it because it is so genuine. To feel the church has to do with the genuineness of our dealings with the Lord, in which we have allowed Him to gain us in one area of our heart after another. In 1 Peter 1:22 this principle is expressed: "Since you have purified your souls by your obedience to the truth unto unfeigned brotherly love, love one another from a pure heart fervently."

Now that we have seen Paul's prayer in Ephesians 3, let us look at his words in Ephesians 6. When speaking of the slaves being obedient to their masters he says, "Not with eye-service as men-pleasers but as slaves of Christ, doing the will of God from the soul" (v. 6). The Greek word here for soul is *psuche;* and the Greek preposition preceding soul is *ek*, meaning "out of." Thus, Paul admonishes the believers to do the will of God "out of" or "out from" the source of their soul. This means doing the will of God with feelings from our soul that are mingled with God's own feelings.

In Philippians 1:8 Paul says, "For God is my witness how I long after you all *in the inward parts of Christ Jesus*." This can also be literally translated "in the bowels of Christ Jesus." Thus, Paul is full of mingled feelings when he says to the Philippians, "I long after you all in the bowels of Christ Jesus." What is this? This is a man who felt the church in his inward parts. It is not merely a program to go visit people. It is not merely setting aside a weeknight to make calls on church members. This is not what Paul is describing. This is living with and feeling the burden for the saints and for others. If we do not experience the Lord in our daily life, if we are not strengthened into our inner man so that Christ may make His home in our heart, then to us the church becomes a schedule. It becomes perfunctory, it becomes duty, it becomes obligation. In other words, the church does not proceed from the inward parts of Christ.

Then there is the opposite kind of experience — you cannot wait to make a call, you cannot wait to take care of a situation. That is, you feel it. To feel it means Christ is flowing in and from you. His life feels in your feelings. Life is not just a term. It is Christ reacting within my reactions because I have given Him the space in me to do that. He has made home in my heart. But if my heart is riveted to television, if my heart is riveted to sports, if my heart is riveted to *my* job, if my heart is riveted to *my* money, *my* bank account, if my heart is riveted to *my* own pleasures, if my heart is riveted to *my* own goals — either human goals or spiritual goals — if my heart is riveted to *my* this or *my* that, then there cannot be much capacity in me to feel anything for the church. I will feel *only* for myself.

Has God dealt with you in your motives? What is the driving force in your life? What does sports represent in your life? What does money represent in your life? What does your fun represent in your life? Do you have another goal other than God? You say, "Well, I love the Lord. I see the church." But your life tells on you. It tells others that you do not feel the church. If we would experience Christ making our heart single with one life-goal and one life-motive, we would have room for Christ to make home in our hearts to live the church life. The Lord Himself will work into us a church-life disposition. In fact, this is precisely what Paul points out in his prayer in Ephesians 3:14-21 and in his exhortation in Ephesians 4:1-3. To feel the church is not natural to us. It is an imparted disposition that is infused into us by the operation of the Spirit upon our inward parts. This impartation begins in our inner man and moves out to our heart.

There are some believers who are not willing to experience the Lord to the extent of having a heart for Christ and the church. Some do turn away as did the rich young ruler in the Gospels (Matt. 19:16-22; Mark 10:17-22; Luke 18:18-23). He was not willing to follow the Lord by selling all. He was sorrowful. He just did not have the willingness to give up his possessions. Like him, we may see a "mountain" in ourself and say, "Well, I cannot give that up. My heart is riveted to it." This simply means you have become aware of your inability to change yourself.

Realizing your inability to change yourself is necessary. It is the first step. You first enter into the experience of Romans 7. That is, you realize you are wretched and you cannot do anything to change yourself. But there is Another life in you, and the power of this resurrection life can operate from within to change your unwillingness. So if you will just be willing to be made willing, this is all the Lord needs. It is a matter of simply opening to the Lord and saying, "Lord, make me willing in my heart," and then trusting Him to do it.

But some are not even willing to offer that prayer. If you are not, then you will remain at a stalemate in your Christian life. You may go on living your own life and having your own way for another year or two, but eventually God in His love will send some environments (Heb. 12:6). God will come and knock at your door once again, touching your money, touching your pleasure-seeking, touching your sports, touching your everything. Why? Because God begins a work and He finishes it. So we have to say, "Amen, Lord." He is going to have His way eventually, so we might as well let Him have His way now. We can save ourself from all the troubles by simply yielding and saying, "Lord Jesus, I love You. Have Your way in me, Lord. Operate in me. Thank You, Jesus."

The more you experience the Lord in this way, the more something will happen in you. You will become one who loves the church with the affections of your heart. You will be just like Jesus. He loved the church and He gave Himself for her! He is the merchant in the parable in Matthew 13:45-46 that found the pearl of great price — the church! And He went and sold all, and He bought it. This is how much the church can mean to us because we have the same

Christ in us who loves that way. He is going to impart *that* love into many people. They will become people who are just like Christ — expressing Him and loving what the Father loves. Christ loves His house. He loves His Body.

We can enter into the revelation that Paul prayed for in Ephesians 1 in a moment's time. We may be hearing a message about eternity past, eternity future, and God's purpose being worked out in time through the church. By simply hearing this word, you may respond by saying, "Hallelujah, I have seen the church!" This is like a honeymoon experience. Then, after the honeymoon, comes the daily life where you really live, where your heart really is. Here you experience the Lord, and in experiencing Him you are brought into your inner man. Then the Lord touches you about something in your life, and you say, "Amen, God." This is how the Lord has His way, how He makes home in our hearts.

According to the tenses in the Greek text, Christ making home in our hearts is simultaneous with our being rooted and grounded in love (Eph. 3:17). Then we are able to apprehend with all the saints. We have a capacity for saint-life — for church life. We are filled with all the fullness of God. Oh, this is to feel the church! It takes our hearts to feel the church. It has everything to do with our hearts. So we have to say, "Lord, do the work in our hearts."

Now, let us look at the work God does in the motives of our heart. Second Corinthians 1:12 says, "For our boasting is this, the testimony of our conscience, that in singleness and sincerity of God, not in fleshly wisdom but in the grace of God, we have conducted ourselves in the world, and more abundantly toward you." Paul uses the terms "singleness" and "sincerity of God." The word "sincerity" means genuineness. This refers to the genuineness and the sincerity of God. Paul is talking about his relationship with the saints. He recognized that his genuineness, his sincerity, his singleness, and his faithfulness to those saints was something out of the source of God Himself.

It is so precious when the divine work has reached our heart and soul to the extent that Christ can be conveyed between us. Another person feels for you, prays for you, and is concerned about your well-being and how you are going on in the Lord. This is because there is room, there is capacity, in that person's heart for others. If there is no singleness in our heart, there is not much capacity except for ourselves and our things. Paul prayed the way he did in Ephesians 3 because he knew that to have the church you have to have people who feel it. And for people to feel it, they have to experience the Lord. They must have dealings with God in their lives. There must be some divine activity going on. Then it is genuine and real. It is not a performance. It is not a show. It is not our "setting up shop" to have the church. No, the church must be Christ through and through, experienced by us. Indeed, the church proceeds from Christ Himself.

One spirit and one soul

In Philippians 1:27 we see where our feelings for the church are located in us. Paul says, "Only, conduct yourselves in a manner worthy of the gospel of Christ, that whether coming and seeing you or being absent, I may hear of the things concerning you, that you stand firm *in one spirit, with one soul* striving together along with the faith of the gospel." Invariably the translators will translate this as "in one spirit and one mind." But the Greek text says, "in one spirit, with one soul *[psuche]*." What Paul is saying is simply to stand together in your spirits, and then your souls will all be blended together. In other words, the effects of being one spirit will reach your soul.

Then Paul says, "striving together." The word striving comes from the compound Greek word *sunathleo* (συναθλέω), from which we derive the word athlete. The Greek word means "coordinating together like a team" and could be expressed as "teaming together." For example, there are some basketball players who are very individualistic in their playing. But there are others who are team players and coordinate well with the rest of the team. On a basketball team you have to learn to "team together" in a coordinated way. In the same way, in the church life when we stand together in one spirit, we will also "team together" with one soul. There is a blending of our spirits and our souls. We feel together. We think together. We choose together. Thus, we conduct ourselves in a coordinated way for the sake of the gospel and the church life.

Coordination in prayer is a good example of this blending. A brother recently commented concerning a prayer meeting. He said, "It seems like when anyone prays, he repeats what everyone else says. Shouldn't we each just have an individual prayer?" What the brother observed was that someone prayed, and after he prayed, another person entered right into his prayer and picked up the same burden and began to pray with that burden. I said to the brother, "Have you ever seen the four living creatures in the first chapter of Ezekiel?" In this account there were four living creatures and they all had wings that touched each other. One of the living creatures faced out in one direction with his wings spread out. The second living creature faced out in another direction with his wings spread out. And the third and fourth living creatures faced out in two different directions with their wings spread out. Again, all four living creatures' wings were touching one another.

These four living creatures represent God's move on the earth. More specifically, they reveal the oneness and coordination in God's move through the prayers of the saints. They were not only attached together by their wings touching one another, but their movement was a movement of one entity. Ezekiel 1:9 says, "Their wings touched one another. The creatures did not turn when they went, but each one went straight forward." Whatever direction one of them moved, the other three followed without turning their faces. When the spirit moved one of the living creatures to go in one direction, they all moved together in that direction (v. 12). This outward example in the Old Testament is a graphic description of what takes place inwardly in the realm of the spirit when the members of the Body of Christ coordinate together in prayer.

When we pray together in one spirit we experience being one soul. Because we are members of the same one Body, when one member has a burden, the other members feel the same burden and move together to bear it. Paul comments on this spiritual phenomenon in 1 Corinthians 12:25-26: [25b] "but that the members would have the same care for one another. [26] And whether one member suffers, all the members suffer with it; or one member is glorified, all the members rejoice with it."

When you feel the church in your experience, you apprehend with all saints the many dimensions and directions of Christ. You do not always need a separate, personal leading when you are a person who feels the church. We move together with other members in one spirit, with one soul. This is the reality of the church being built in our experience. When we are related and built up with the other members, we receive the rich supply of Christ, the Head, coming through every joint and band (Eph.

4:16; Col. 2:19). This is the reality in God's building. You begin to realize that your Christian life was not meant to be individualistic. "In one spirit, with one soul" indicates that when we genuinely touch the spirit together, there is oneness in our soul. Oneness in soul is a matter of feeling the burdens together and coordinating together in a practical church life.

Feeling the oneness of the church

The apostle Paul says in Philippians 2:1-2, [1] "If there is therefore any encouragement in Christ, if any consolation of love, if any fellowship of spirit, if any tenderheartedness and compassions, [2] make my joy full, that you think the same thing, having the same love, joined in soul, thinking the one thing." Then in verse 3 he says, "Doing nothing by way of selfish ambition nor by way of vainglory, but in lowliness of mind considering one another more excellent than yourselves." Now, as we continue to read Philippians 2, let us stay in the context and think with Paul. That is, we should restrict our mind to Paul's thought and not think outside of his context. In verse 14 he says, "Do all things without murmurings and reasonings." What he was burdened for was that the saints would sense or feel any intrusion that came against the oneness of the church in the form of murmurings and reasonings. This exhortation is not merely an isolated, ethical command. It is based upon the fact that God was actively operating in the saints. Verse 13 says, "For it is God who operates in you both the willing and the working for His good pleasure." Paul wants them to feel how precious the oneness in the church life is to God. In this verse he even identifies this oneness as "God's good pleasure."

To feel the church life is to feel that the slightest murmuring or reasoning against the saints is interfering with God's operation within us. When we feel the church the way the apostle Paul did, the slightest reasoning of our mind about a brother or sister will be regarded as an attack on the oneness of the Spirit. But if we can remain in our critical thoughts for days without dealing with the Lord, this means we do not genuinely feel the church according to the divine value.

Feeling the things of the church

Philippians 2:19-20 presents an example of a man who felt the church. Paul says, [19] "But I hope in the Lord Jesus to send Timothy to you shortly, that I also may be encouraged by knowing the things concerning you. [20] For I have no one like-souled who will genuinely care for what concerns you." To be like-souled means that we have the same burdens, the same feelings, and the same heart about the things of the church.

Then Paul presents the contrast in verse 21: "For all seek their own things, not the things of Christ Jesus." Man, when left to himself, will live for and seek his own things. We know what it is to selfishly live for our own things. Again, if we do not deal with the Lord over our selfish heart and habits, we will not be capable of feeling the church in a practical way. We will only make time and room to take care of our own things. However, if in our lives we have any experience of Christ touching the deep roots of our self-life, the natural outcome will be that we make room for not only Christ, but for "the things of Christ Jesus." To have care and feeling for the things of Christ Jesus as Timothy did is expressed in caring for the practical affairs of the church life, including the practical needs of the saints.

When we are like-souled we not only have one spirit, but we have one heart and one soul. This is not because of human psychology or effort. It is because we are all passing through experiences of Christ, and our hearts are all dealt with in the same kind of way. We tell the Lord, "Lord, I have no other goal but one — You Yourself." God Himself with His purpose is our one unique goal. When God is the goal of our life, then our life becomes very simple. Everything is equal. Whether we feel happy or sad, whether we are passing through a rough environment or a smooth environment, it all means one thing — that we may gain Christ and be found in Him. When we experience Christ in our lives in this kind of way, there is a settling down of Christ in us. He makes home in our hearts. Then we know the church not only by the enlightenment of revelation, but also by experiential apprehension and feeling. This apprehending comes as our heart is dealt with by the Lord and we make it a place exclusively for Christ.

May the Holy Spirit continue to speak much more to us through this fellowship concerning our seeing and feeling the church. And may we all respond to His speaking by opening our hearts to "Him who is able to do superabundantly above all that we ask or think, according to the power which operates in us" (Eph. 3:20).

3 ▶ A Church-Life Disposition

Seeing the church is in the realm of revelation

N o one can know what the church is in a natural way. In Ephesians 3:3-6 the church is referred to as "the mystery of Christ." A mystery in Scripture is something that is made known only by revelation from God and not by man's natural thought or wisdom (1 Cor. 2:7-10). Therefore, the church, being a mystery, can be understood only in the realm of revelation. This means that the church is not known in a common way. The church is not a matter left for man to figure out by his cleverness. Neither is the church in the category of investigation or theological debate. The church is in the category of revelation. Thus, to see the church, we must see it according to the ministry of the New Testament apostles.

The apostle Paul prayed in Ephesians 1 based upon the principle that the church cannot be known apart from revelation. His prayer was that all believers would have a spirit of wisdom and revelation in the full knowledge of God, with the eyes of their heart enlightened to see and to know what the church is. When the church is opened up in this way, we discover that it is God's creation, God's masterpiece, God's product. The church is what He created (Eph. 2:10, 15; 4:24; Col. 3:10; Gal. 6:15). It is what He brought into existence through Christ's death and resurrection. The church is "the new man," created in the realm of the new creation. It is the very Body of Christ made up of members who are being filled with the One who fills all in all (Eph. 1:23). As His Body, the church is the expression of the fullness of Christ.

The church in the Bible is something that originates from God, not man. This is a principle similar to the principle of salvation. The way of salvation is not something we devise or make up; nor is it something optional, as though we have a "say" in the matter. When it comes to the way of salvation, we have no choice. The plan of salvation has been entirely conceived by God. Therefore, it is in the realm of revelation. When the gospel is preached, it comes as something unveiled to us by God. The gospel is the revelation of *God's plan* for redemption, not *our ideas* about redemption. The revelation of the gospel generates faith in us to believe in Christ and be saved.

The way we regard salvation is exactly the way we should regard the church. The church is not something we create. The church is not in the realm of alternatives. We are not given a choice about the kind of church we want. The church has nothing to do with man's choice, man's opinions, or man's preferences. The church is in the realm of God's choice.

We do not join the church as though it were an organization. The church is not something you become a member of by signing your name to a membership roll. We become the church when we become children of God (Acts 2:41, 47). And we become children of God by being born again, or regenerated (1 Pet. 1:3; Titus 3:5). Through regeneration we become organically joined to Christ, our living Head. Thus, we become the church by our new birth and by Christ, our life, indwelling us. That is why in the New Testament the believers were identified simply as "the church" in the various cities where they lived. They were not denominational churches or groups of Christians gathered around doctrines, methods, or men. The churches in the book of Acts, in the Epistles, and in Revelation were composed of members of Christ begotten by the Spirit, baptized in the Spirit into one Body (1 Cor.

12:13), and existing together in the Spirit (Eph. 4:3-4). The churches were not divided, with different party names. They were simply what they were according to spiritual reality. They were "the churches of Christ," that is, local expressions of the living Christ (Rom. 16:16).

Thus, in the New Testament we read of "the church in Jerusalem," "the church in Philadelphia," "the church in Laodicea," and "the churches of Galatia." All you could do was identify the church according to *where it was.* That is all! The unique identification of the church in the New Testament was geographical! It was not identified in a denominational way; neither was it identified in a way that shifted its focus to someone or something other than Christ. Universally, the church was one. Locally and practically, the church was one. This was because the church, to the New Testament believers, was in the realm of God's choice rather than man's choice.

When we see the church in the same way the New Testament believers saw the church, we can no longer be "church shoppers." It is no longer a matter of trying out this group or that group, according to our likes and dislikes. When we see the church by revelation, we realize it is for keeps! We are not experimenting to see whether or not we like "the program" or the believers we meet with. Oh, brothers and sisters, the church is far deeper than that. Christ died on the cross for keeps! (Eph. 2:13-18). He produced the church in resurrection for keeps! (Eph. 1:19-23). When we see the church by revelation, we have a deep sense that it is for keeps! Paul's prayer in Ephesians 1 is precisely that all believers would know the church in the realm of revelation, and experience it for keeps.

Experiencing the church is in
the realm of an infused disposition

After we realize that seeing the church is not something natural, we also need to realize that experiencing the practical church life is not something natural. According to Paul's prayer in Ephesians 3, it is clear that the kind of church life he opens up in chapters 4—6 requires an infused disposition, or what may be called a church-life disposition. The church life cannot be practiced according to man's flesh or natural, soulish life. For instance, the believers in Corinth experienced many problems because they were living in their fleshliness and soulishness while meeting as the church in that city (1 Cor. 2:14—3:4).

According to the divine estimation, the old man, the flesh, and the self are just not able to live the church life. To live the church life on this earth does not, so to speak, come naturally to us. It demands that we all be under the infusion of a higher life and a higher disposition. It is a life and disposition other than our own. Because of this, Paul prays in Ephesians 3 for the resurrection power to so operate in us that Christ Himself would make home in our hearts, becoming our very disposition to live the church life (Eph. 3:16-21).

The evidence that Christ has made His home in our heart is that we have the capacity to feel the church in our heart. As we partake of Christ's disposition, we become persons who feel the church. It is in our care. It is in our thought. It is in our feeling. We not only see the church by revelation, but *our heart is in the church.* There is in us an imparted aptitude for the church life. This comes from experiencing the inner power of the resurrected Christ that produces a church-life disposition (Eph. 3:20; 2 Pet. 1:4).

Paul's prayer in Ephesians 3 is that we would feel the church in our disposition. This prayer is answered gradually in most of our lives. The more we allow the Lord to occupy our heart, the more we will feel His feelings for the church. We are all in the process. There are areas of our heart that the Lord has gained. There are areas that He is presently working on, and there are areas unknown to our present consciousness that He will touch in the future. But throughout this process, there is among us one common aim — to gain Christ every step of the way.

When we touch the genuine church life we may feel somewhat uncomfortable. This is because the undealt-with self does not fit in the church. In my own experience, when I first touched the church life I felt exposed. My natural life and self was laid bare for what it was. The light shining in all the saints made me realize that my seminary experience did not matter here. What I thought I knew did not matter. Reputation or eloquence did not count. What mattered was Christ! Can you impart something of Christ? Can you flow out Christ to others from your spirit? What measure of Christ can you share? Do you experience Christ? The saints' common orientation to the realm of the spirit automatically makes manifest what is Christ and what is not Christ.

Having those initial feelings of uncomfortableness, I now realize, was exactly as it should be. When the church is proper, it is a place where the secrets of our heart become manifest (1 Cor. 14:24-25). It is true, our undealt-with self is not welcome in the church. Whenever this self or natural energy or fleshly opinion touches the church, there is a counter-reaction within the spirits of "the saints in the light" (Col. 1:12). This reaction is an inward repelling of everything that is not Christ. There is simply no "Amen" in the corporate consciousness of the saints. This is not a matter of being rude or impolite according to social ethics. It is a matter of the consciousness of the church recognizing only one kind of disposition for the church life — the disposition of Christ (Phil. 2:5, Weymouth). The church only cares for Christ. Christ is all and in all! Therefore, whenever the self-life is exposed and manifested, it is a sign of a proper and healthy church. (See the account of Ananias and Sapphira in Acts 5:1-11.)

When we have a genuine experience of Christ making home in our heart, we will discover that there is a disposition to live the church life. We are strengthened into our inner man, and the result is that we are able or full of strength to apprehend with all the saints the knowledge-surpassing love of Christ. That is, we receive an infused disposition. This disposition is wrought into us to live out a practical church life where there is the need to keep the oneness of the Spirit in the bond of peace (Eph. 3:20—4:3). To meet together with all different kinds of believers at different stages of growth in the Lord goes beyond the capacity of our natural disposition. It requires a supernatural disposition. By this infused disposition we can be built up together in the knowledge-surpassing love of Christ.

If we really see by revelation the kind of church that is revealed in the book of Ephesians, we will realize that our natural disposition could never make it. We need divine enablement. It is only by Christ making home in our heart that we could be rooted and grounded in love to the extent that we have supernatural ability to apprehend the vast dimensions of Christ's love in the church.

According to Ephesians 5, for the Lord to gain the church as His Bride, there is the need of an infusion of the divine disposition into our disposition. To live the church life together requires the divine nature and disposition. No one is naturally born "cut out" for the church life. The church life demands Another life. This is why the Lord told Nicodemus in John 3 that in order to *see* the kingdom of God, as well as to *enter* the kingdom of God, it was necessary to be born again. Seeing and entering the kingdom is virtually the same as seeing and entering the church life (Rom. 14:17). The church life is altogether a matter of Another life coming into us through regeneration, and then of our being constantly infused with the disposition that is in that life.

Living the church life is based upon Another life rather than our natural life. This should be very encouraging to us all. It means that it is within the reach of all of us. No one is excluded. There is no such thing as some being born with "church-life ability" and others being born without it. No! The church life described in the New Testament is so transcendent and so out of reach to the natural life that nothing but the divine disposition can live it. Thus, instead of the Lord leaving the church life to our natural disposition, He crucified us, joined us to Himself in resurrection, and became one with our spirit. By doing this, He pulled us away from ourselves and redirected us to do one thing — to become a partaker of the divine nature (2 Pet. 1:3-4; Heb. 3:1, 14; 1 Cor. 1:9). It is by this daily partaking of Him that we participate in His life and are spontaneously infused with His disposition.

This is not only an encouragement to us, but it also takes away all our excuses for not living the church life. If your excuse is that you are not willing for the church life, then God promises to work the very willingness of His disposition into you (Phil. 2:5, 12-13). If you cannot imagine yourself being absolute for the church life, then He quickly whisks you away from the tyranny of that thought to a secret power working within your spirit (Eph. 3:16). It is that power that is able to do exceedingly abundantly above all that we ask or think (Eph. 3:20). If you feel that you do not have a heart for the church, that too is okay; the Lord already knew that (Ezek. 36:26). What He does for your heartlessness over the church is take the pressure off by removing your anxiety about your condition. He does this by simply inviting Himself into your heart to make His home there (Rev. 3:20; Eph. 3:17). Then your heart is no longer the same heart. His occupying of your heart brings with it a whole new set of feelings and reactions, and you discover that you have new feelings for the church. This is the infusion of a church-life disposition.

Under the apostles' New Testament ministry, feeling the church was a matter of infusion. But today in the religious world, feeling the church is a different matter. It is often merely in the realm of pastors and church leaders trying to pressure and influence people to make a commitment to the church. That is why there are so many leadership and motivational seminars in the Christian world. Everyone is scurrying around to learn some new technique on how to motivate their people.

Of course, this is not according to what is revealed in the life and ministry of the early believers. The church in the New Testament was not motivated by techniques. The church was a matter of all the saints learning to partake of the unsearchable riches of Christ. By this partaking Christ Himself could then build His own church from within the spirits and hearts of the saints by an infusion of His disposition (Matt. 16:18; 1 Pet. 2:2-3, 5). Lack of commitment is a symptom of a lack of life, not a lack of motivational techniques. If there is no heart to feel the church, that means that Christ has not made His home in the saints' hearts. The need is not to try to prop things up by persuasion and methods, but to bow our knees to enter into Paul's prayer in Ephesians 3.

The way the Lord feels about the church is described in Matthew 13:45-46. In this parable, the merchant finds the pearl of great price and goes and sells all to buy it. This unveils how deep the Lord's feelings and value are for the church. In Ephesians 5:25 Paul unveils this same kind of feeling when he says that Christ "loved the church and gave Himself up for her." Christ is now sanctifying the church, cleansing her, nourishing and cherishing her. One day He will present the church to Himself all glorious within. This glorious inner work is described in Psalm 45:13-14. Here the king's daughter is brought to him in a garment that is made of fine needlework. This needlework is the fine stitching work of the Holy Spirit taking place in our daily lives. It is also the same as the fine linen garment of the wife of the Lamb mentioned in Revelation 19:7-8. This fine linen garment does not represent Christ as our *imputed righteousness* in a positional way (1 Cor. 1:30), but Christ as our *imparted righteousness* in a dispositional way. This means that in our experience the Lord has so worked in us in a corporate way, that we are presented to Him with the highest expression of His grace — a beautifully stitched garment that has been completely wrought by the Spirit — a church-life disposition. Our thinking, our feelings, our choices, our relationships, are all mingled with Christ's disposition.

Seeing the power to produce a church-life disposition

The apostle Paul's prayer in Ephesians 1 includes a petition not only for enlightenment to see God's plan for the church, but also for enlightenment to see the power that produces the church. To see that God wants the church is one thing; to see the power that can produce the church is another. For the church to come into existence, there is the need for power — resurrection power. Resurrection power alone can produce the church that God requires.

This power operates first upon our spirit to resurrect it from the dead and make it alive together with Christ (Eph. 2:1, 5-6). Then the power operates upon our heart for Christ to make home there, and to produce a disposition rooted and grounded in love (Eph. 3:16-17). It is this disposition which enables us to apprehend with all the saints the knowledge-surpassing love of Christ (vv. 18-19). The power is so effective in its operation that it can go beyond what we ask or think to the extent of producing glory in the church! (vv. 20-21).

The power revealed in the book of Ephesians is not power to perform signs and wonders; rather, it is power that forms within us a disposition that can live a practical church life. Thus, after the apostle Paul speaks of "the power which operates in us" at the end of Ephesians 3, he defines what he means by "power." In Ephesians 4:1-3 he says, [1] "I beseech you therefore, I, the prisoner in the Lord, to walk worthily of the calling with which you were called, [2] with all lowliness and meekness, with long-suffering, bearing one another in love, [3] being diligent to keep the oneness of the Spirit in the uniting bond of peace." On the positive side, we can see that the power issues in a disposition that has been dealt with by God. This disposition manifests the virtues that are necessary to live the church life — lowliness of mind, meekness, endurance, and forbearance in love. On the negative side, these virtues imply that our natural life and disposition have undergone some dealings and breakings.

The power that raised Christ from the dead in Ephesians 1 is now operating to subdue our self-life, which is expressed in highmindedness, pride, defensiveness, impatience, self-seeking, and selfishness. We can no longer remain an unbroken person who fortifies himself with reasonings and self-conceit. In the church life, if we are a "whole person," full of pride and self-trust, we will find ourselves in troublesome relationships that negatively affect the church. The reason for this is that our undealt-with self does not fit in the church. Only Christ experienced by us fits in the church (Col. 3:10-11).

When the church is in a proper state, the undealt-with self will feel uncomfortable and even unhappy with the church. If a brother or sister does not receive mercy to be dealt with under the mighty hand of God, they will inevitably merge with their undealt-with thoughts and feelings. Whenever a person merges with his unbroken self-life, he becomes an instrument of Satan to blame and even attack the church. This is what happened to the apostle Peter in the incident recorded in Matthew 16:21-25. Peter's undealt-with self, expressed through his opinion about the Lord going to the cross, became a direct attack of Satan upon the Lord.

It is important to expose the behavior of the undealt-with self in the church. It conceals itself under the guise of being treated unfairly. It blames.

It finds fault. It feels neglected. It reacts in the most subtle ways to get others to side with it. It will vindicate itself in any way it can. All of these reactions are examples of the devious ways the undealt-with self seeks to camouflage itself. Unfortunately, the person who merges and takes sides with his self-life is often ignorant that his reasoning mind is only a cloak for the undealt-with self. The fruit of a self-life not dealt with by God is often manifested in relationships. Indeed, our relationships with one another reveal how much of the disposition of Christ is actually in us (cf. Phil. 2:3-5, 12-14).

If our self-life is not dealt with, we become a magnanimous person. The word "magnanimous" comes from a compound Latin word that literally means "great-souled." To be magnanimous means to be a great person outwardly. It can be compared to a politician who seeks to please everyone. It means to be a big-souled person who can get along with everyone. A magnanimous person will have a smile on his face while secretly holding strong opinions, arguments, and disagreements. Thus, a magnanimous person appears outwardly to go along with everyone, but inwardly he is filled up with opinions that are covered and held down. The opinions are not dealt with by the cross. Instead of dealing and interacting with God, a magnanimous person will suppress his feelings. Somehow he can say "Praise the Lord" with his lips while allowing dissenting thoughts to fester within. This may last for a while in the church life, but eventually something will happen to expose the strong opinions and dissenting thoughts. The more a person keeps things within and copes with them instead of dealing with God, the more his self-life grows bigger and bigger.

We must realize that in the church life there is only one destiny for the self — crucifixion. There are no back doors, fire escapes, or exits. There is just termination — the termination of the self. This is not negative; it is very positive. Who wants this old self anyway? It has controlled us and made us miserable. Because of this self, we cannot get along with people. We are even unhappy with ourselves. Why? Because we have an undealt-with self-life.

Jeremiah 17:9-10 says, [9] "The heart is deceitful above all things, and desperately wicked; who can know it? [10a] I, the LORD, search the heart, I test the mind." These verses clearly indicate that none of us can know our heart. Thus, in dealing with the Lord to allow His resurrection power to change us, we simply must learn to drop ourselves and trust ourselves wholly to Him. And as we come to know Him in His light, we see light. That light shines upon us, and then we look at the self from a different point of view. It is no longer a matter of condemnation. It is not in that realm. It is in the realm of loathing and nausea (Ezek. 36:31). We learn to take sides with God against ourself. We are not threatened by our ugliness and fallen disposition, because we know it is a crucified thing. There is a dividing of our soul and spirit, allowing us to see the soul for what it is. We no longer defend it, excuse it, or vindicate it.

Thus, the divine power operating in us is designed to break down the self-life and to produce the disposition of Christ in our hearts. Then there will be a genuine church life with an apprehension of the knowledge-surpassing love of Christ. This means we actually love one another *in* His love — we love one another *the way* Christ loves us. That love flows in us, passes through us, and causes glory to be in the church.

It is the reality of this love that makes the church the fullness of the One who fills all in all. This fullness expressed through the members is produced gradually by our growing up into Christ in all things.

A church-life disposition is formed in each member until there is "a full-grown man, at the measure of the stature of the fullness of Christ" (Eph. 4:13, 15-16). This is the burden of Paul's second prayer for the believers, recorded in Ephesians 3.

Oh, brothers and sisters, there is power operating in us to produce a disposition to live the church life. This power is able to transform us so that we live out the virtues of Christ — lowliness of mind, meekness, endurance, and forbearance. Forbearance literally means "to put up with one another." Of course, Paul adds "in love." This is a bearing of one another in the love of God. That means there is divine love flowing in my disposition toward you. Instead of merely tolerating one another in our self-life, the Lord gives us a different taste and a different attitude in our dispositions. We are sweetened with Christ. We express Christ. The power of God is working in us to produce this kind of disposition, because it is only this kind of disposition that can keep the oneness of the Spirit in the uniting bond of peace.

The purpose of the power is to produce the church, that is, to produce a church-life disposition. The nature of the power is resurrection power, all-transcending power. It is the power that caused

Christ to be raised far above all. He transcended the evil angelic rulers and authorities. This power raised Him from the tomb, propelled Him through the atmosphere, took Him to the heavenlies, and set Him at the Father's right hand. Also, it is all-subduing power. By it, He subjected all things under His feet. This power made Him Lord, Christ, and Head over all things to the church.

It is this power that Paul prayed for us to see. It was as though Paul was saying to the believers, "Don't worry about your condition. Don't worry about your pride. Don't worry about your heart. Don't look at the apparently insurmountable things in your life. Stop for a moment! Look at the power that is to the church. It's resurrection power! It's all-transcending power! It's all-subduing power! And it's heading-up power! It made Christ the Head. He became Head over all things to the church." Now, it is this very same power that is being transmitted into our spirit. This power is now declared to be "to the church." This means there is a transmission of this power into our spirit, into our heart, and into our relationships. This power is intended to produce the church, His masterpiece (Eph. 2:10).

So, brothers and sisters, there must be reality in

the church. But it is reality among imperfect people who are all in the process. That is why having a disposition for the church life is particularly related to being flooded with the love of Christ. Having the knowledge-surpassing love of Christ is having a love that goes beyond what we can ask or think. The very fact that the Word says "knowledge-surpassing" means it is something beyond the limitation of our thoughts toward one another. It is a release of the divine love. It is Calvary love being released from the dispositions of the saints. It is enjoying *that* love — love that is able to swallow up all the negative things.

To feel the church in our experience is to open our heart fully to the Lord. As we invite Him to make home in our heart, He produces in it a disposition that can live the church life. This disposition is just Christ. Our prayer is, "Lord, keep working to terminate the self. I don't care if it raises its ugly head. Just go ahead, Lord, and keep working. Even though it may seem painful at times, I thank You, Lord, that You have not left me to myself. Thank You that You have allowed so many troubles in my life to exasperate me and to let this self come out in the open so that it can be dealt with by the cross. By Your resurrection power, subdue me and transform me, that I might have the same disposition that is in You for the sake of the church!"

4 ▶ The Willingness of the Church

How glorious it is that on this earth the willingness of the Lord Jesus could be embodied in His people — that is, His willingness in living unto the Father's good pleasure could be transmitted into His Body. The transmission of this willingness is possible because we are members of Him, joined organically to Him as our Head. Thus, we participate in the very disposition of Christ in the form of willingness. This willingness is transmitted, embodied, and expressed corporately. It is expressed practically and visibly so that it can be known and seen. The church existing in this age is actually the testimony of Jesus, where the very life of the Lord is embodied in a unique and special way — in our willingness to serve one another.

The corporate testimony of willingness

God's move throughout the Bible was always a move based upon one major principle, the willingness of His people. He would not do anything apart from the willingness embodied in His people. This

is seen particularly related to His corporate testimony with the tabernacle under Moses, the temple
under David and Solomon, and the recovered temple
under Ezra and Nehemiah. In the three sections of the
Old Testament describing the tabernacle, the temple,
and the recovered temple, one common thing is mentioned — the willingness of the people in serving the
Lord to build His corporate testimony. The Lord's
testimony always expressed itself in His people's
willingness to live for God's pleasure on the earth.

> *God is known on the earth*
> *in His people's willingness*

We can see that the Lord embodies Himself and
makes Himself known on the earth. The way He
testifies of Himself to the earth is expressed in John
13:34-35: [34] "A new commandment I give to you,
that you love one another, as I have loved you, that
you also love one another. [35] By this all will know
that you are My disciples, if you have love for one
another." These verses tell us that all men are going
to know who God's people are. There is going to be
a testimony that is visible and touchable. How will
this testimony be made known? There will be groups

of saints in city after city over the whole earth who have a willingness, embodied in their relationships, to live unto the Lord and to serve Him and one another. This willingness is the expression of the divine love flowing out.

God makes Himself known by His people's willingness to live for His house. It is not "going to church." It is not attending a certain church meeting out of obligation or in a perfunctory way. It is not just token attendance, token giving, or token serving, but a welling up of Another life — a life that is consumed for the Father's house. The genuineness of the testimony of the church today on this earth is embodied in the experience of willingness.

Now let us see how this willingness becomes embodied in God's people. Psalm 110:1-4 says, [1] "The LORD said to my Lord, Sit at My right hand, till I make Your enemies Your footstool. [2] The LORD shall send the rod of Your strength out of Zion. Rule in the midst of Your enemies! [3] Your people shall be volunteers in the day of Your power; in the beauties of holiness, from the womb of the morning, You have the dew of Your youth. [4] The LORD has sworn and will not relent, You are a priest forever according to the order of Melchizedek." The *Amplified Bible* renders verse 3, "Your people will offer themselves willingly in the day of Your power, in the beauty of holiness and in holy array out of the womb of the morning; to You will spring forth Your young men who are as the dew." The first part of this verse tells us that in the day of the Lord's power, His people will offer themselves willingly.

What is "the day of Your power"? It is the day of Christ as our High Priest according to the order of Melchizedek. Our High Priest has passed through human life, crucifixion, resurrection, ascension, enthronement, and lordship, and He is now ever living to make intercession for us, to transmit the victory of His life into us. We are the recipients of the transmission of an indestructible life that is pulsating through our being, dealing with and tearing down every blockage and hindrance in our heart, softening our hard heart. This is because the very life of God is filling us. And all this is happening because Christ is interceding. He is praying it into being. The day of His power refers to His present intercession by which He is transmitting into our spirits His very life and nature. Thus to say, "Your people will offer themselves willingly *in the day of Your power,*" means "in the day that You are on the throne, interceding and transmitting Your very life and nature into our being."

Brothers and sisters, all willingness in our being, whether it is much or a little, is the direct result of the intercession of our Melchizedek, who is transmitting His resurrected, ascended life into us. This transmission is delivering us from the love of this world, from our attachment to other things, from idols in our heart, from a self-centered life — from every realm where the enemy usurps us. And we are being reduced to God Himself, to love Him, to be single for Him, to be ones who are actually in alignment with the very thing that is on His heart — His building, His habitation. This is our Christ, who is creating the willingness within us for His house.

So we can see from Psalm 110 that in the day of His power there is a willingness. This willingness is an inner feeling: "Lord, when are we going to have another church meeting? I want to be with the saints. I don't want to watch TV. I don't want to go to the movies. I don't even want to take a vacation. I love the church!" What is this? This is the willingness, Christ Himself, surfacing in His people today.

God's desire is to have a corporate testimony of Christ, but not Christ in a general way. It is Christ in the form of His disposition of willingness within the members of His Body. The church is not a forced thing. You do not sign a membership roll. You are not committed or obligated by an outward piece of paper. There is nothing but the disposition of Christ operating in power in us. This is the willingness of Christ Himself within us (Phil. 2:5, 12-13).

Willingness in building the tabernacle

In Exodus 25:2 the Lord said to Moses, "Speak to the children of Israel, that they bring Me an offering. From everyone who gives it willingly with his heart you shall take My offering." Then in verse 8 He says, "And let them make Me a sanctuary, that I may dwell among them." Together these verses reveal that the Lord puts a condition upon the nature of the building of His sanctuary. He actually specifies the nature of how it should take place. All the items were to be offered willingly for that corporate testimony of God's dwelling place. "Everyone who gives . . . willingly with his heart" indicates that the church is not a place to complain about or be obligated to. The church is a place for those who want to be here, for those who are happy to come and willingly give, serve, love, and pour out (Phil. 2:17). It is never a matter of being forced or compelled. You simply cannot help yourself because the nature in you is that way. This is the church.

It is a sorry situation whenever pastors or leaders try to force people to be committed or try to hold a congregation together by methods or ways. The very nature of God's move has nothing to do with the realm of coercing. It has everything to do with a group of people participating in the life of another Person who is absolutely willing — "I delight to do Your will, O my God" (Psa. 40:8; cf. Heb. 10:7). This is why willingness is not merely what is described in a dictionary — wanting to do something or free to do something. No, that is the shell. The kernel and life content of willingness is Christ. Willingness is Christ. Just as we see that all the virtues of the fruit of the Spirit are Christ (for example, patience is Christ), so also willingness is Christ. So whenever willingness is in you, you have met Christ in your being. You have met Him in the form of His disposition of willingness. That is His life. It is the nature of His life within us, the way He feels.

In the Old Testament, when the tabernacle was being constructed, it was done only by those who had a willing heart. In Exodus 35 the building of the tabernacle actually begins to take place. Verse 5 says, "Take from among you an offering to the LORD. Whoever is of a willing heart, let him bring it as an offering to the LORD: gold, silver, and bronze." Again, to offer something to the Lord is not merely an outward act. "Whoever is of a willing heart" reveals the nature of the people's offering, the nature of God's corporate testimony. This is what makes God known on the earth. Willingness in His people makes Him known.

God is not made known in a forced environment, but in an atmosphere of freedom, an atmosphere where willingness can spring forth. This is because love cannot exist without an atmosphere of freedom. Love freely gives. Love freely goes out. Love freely serves. If I put you under a demand to love — "You *must* love me" — that does not express an atmosphere of freedom. That expresses the law of Moses: "Thou shalt . . ." This is the law. What expresses God is an atmosphere of freedom, willingness, and love. This atmosphere characterizes our relationships in the church life.

We see willingness again in Exodus 35:21-29. Verses 21-22 say, [21] "Then everyone came whose heart was stirred, and everyone whose spirit was willing, and they brought the LORD's offering for the work of the tabernacle of meeting, for all its service, and for the holy garments. [22a] They came, both men and women, as many as had a willing heart." Then in verses 22-28 the people brought all the materials for God's house. And the unique characteristic of their offering was "as many as had a willing heart." Then verse 29 says, "The children of Israel brought a freewill offering to the LORD, all the men and women whose hearts were willing to bring material for all kinds of work which the LORD, by the hand of Moses, had commanded to be done." So the entire tabernacle, the corporate testimony of the Lord's move on the earth, was of the nature of willingness.

Now let us see the overflow of willingness in Exodus 36:1-7. Verses 1-3 speak of the people's hearts being lifted up to give to the Lord. And verses 4-7 continue, [4] "Then all the craftsmen who were doing all the work of the sanctuary came, each from the work he was doing, [5] and they spoke to Moses, saying, The people bring much more than enough for the service of the work which the LORD commanded us to do. [6] So Moses gave a commandment, and they caused it to be proclaimed throughout the camp, saying, Let neither man nor woman do any more work for the offering of the sanctuary. And the people were restrained from bringing, [7] for the material they had was sufficient for all the work to be done — indeed too much." Oh, what a testimony of God, that the willingness was to that extent! You had to stop it. Whenever we are experiencing the overflow of this willingness, we literally have to stop the church meetings. Yet all we can do is stop them temporarily for a few hours or until the next day when we can have another meeting. It is this way because of the fullness, because of the overflow that comes from the willingness. This testifies that there is a genuine participation in the life of God. Willingness is the fruit that testifies that God is indeed among us.

Willingness in building the temple

In 1 Chronicles 28 we see willingness in relation to the building of the temple. In the first part of verse 9 David says, "As for you, my son Solomon, know the God of your father, and serve Him with a loyal heart." This can also be translated "with a perfect heart." The Hebrew word indicates a whole heart, a heart that does not have any cracks in it, a heart that is perfect. Then verse 9 continues, "and with a willing *mind.*" The Hebrew word here is *nephesh,* which can also be translated "soul." So it would read "with a willing soul." Here Solomon is exhorted to serve God with a perfect heart and a willing soul. This verse is related to the temple, the corporate testimony. Thus, what the Holy Spirit emphasizes in the building of both the tabernacle and the temple is the word "willing." The corporate testimony must spring from the source of willingness, or there is no testimony of God.

First Chronicles 28:9-10 continues, 9 "for the LORD searches all hearts and understands all the intent of the thoughts. If you seek Him, He will be found by you; but if you forsake Him, He will cast you off forever. 10 Consider now, for the LORD has chosen you to build a house for the sanctuary; be strong, and do it." Together verses 9-10 show us that willingness within our being is specifically related to one thing in God's administration, and that is His house. God's corporate building, more than anything else in your life, will search your heart, your motives, the mainspring of your life, what you live for, what you exist for on this earth. Nothing will search and discern your heart and divide your soul and spirit as much as your relationship to the house of God on this earth. How do you relate to the house of God? Can you take it or leave it? Does it fit into your lifestyle? Is it merely according to your convenience? Is the church merely incidental, a side matter to what you are really doing in your life? Nothing searches the heart and the intents of the heart like the Lord coming to us to live for His house.

God is talking to us. He is saying, "I created the universe for My dwelling place. I made an earth for My people so that I could be their God and live corporately among them, in them, and through them. This is why I made the heavens and the earth. This is why you are a human being. This is why you have a human life on this earth. It is so that you can be a living stone in the Father's house." This is the vision of the universe. It is the unique vision that searches every man. It is not merely about being willing to give up your love for a certain item. It is not just a personal or individual spiritual matter. We may think, "Well, the Lord has dealt with this love, and the Lord has dealt with that love." We may be satisfied with the dealings of God over particular things in our lives. These dealings all have their place, but there is always one major thing that touches the bottom, the spring, of what we live for. Just as we have sung the song, "What will you do with Jesus? Neutral you cannot be," now we can sing, "What will you do with My house? Neutral you cannot be." This means we have dealings in our hearts to such an extent that our plans, our goals, our living, our future, are all wrapped up with His house.

The nature of the life within us is willingness. As this life grows in us and surfaces in us, we find a willingness to live for Christ and the church, a willingness to serve practically for the expression of God's house. Again, 1 Chronicles 28:9 speaks of having a perfect heart, a heart without any blame. Then it tells us that the Lord searches all hearts and understands all the intent of the thoughts or the imaginations. He knows all the thinkings. He knows the motives. God knows the depths of our hearts. Then verse 10 says, "Consider now, for the LORD has chosen you to build a house for the sanctuary; be strong, and do it." Many can personally testify that in coming to the church God dealt with this and that because He was purifying their hearts. Out of this purifying, willingness springs up within us. This willingness is God's life and is the nature of temple life and all the activity related to the temple.

Willingness in the recovery of the temple

In Ezra 1:1-4 a decree went out from Cyrus the king that God's people could go back to Jerusalem and rebuild the temple. So it was possible under the government of that day for them to do it. The Lord opened the way. But even though the way was open, the rebuilding was not automatically going to happen. Yes, the outward environment was there, but God had to find some spirits that were raised up and some hearts that were willing. Otherwise, He could not have the recovery of the building. Verses 5-6 say, [5] "Then the heads of the fathers' houses of Judah and Benjamin, and the priests and the Levites, with all those whose spirits God had moved, arose to go up and build the house of the LORD which is in Jerusalem. [6] And all those who were around them encouraged them with articles of silver and gold, with goods and livestock, and with precious things, besides all that was *willingly* offered." So again, willingness is the nature of the recovery of the temple.

Then Ezra 2:68 says, "Some of the heads of the fathers' houses, when they came to the house of the LORD which is in Jerusalem, offered *freely* for the house of God, to erect it in its place." The word "freely" can also be translated "willingly." Thus, again and again throughout the Old Testament, the characteristic of the corporate testimony is willingness.

Willingness in the early church

In the book of Acts we see the emergence of the church coming out of the whole process the Lord went through — from His incarnation to His ascension to the Spirit's coming and baptizing on the day of Pentecost. The first experience of the church life is recorded in Acts 2. Verses 41-47 give an account of what happened after the Spirit was poured out: [41] "Then those who gladly received his word were baptized; and that day about three thousand souls were added to them. [42] And they continued steadfastly in the apostles' doctrine and fellowship, in the breaking of bread, and in prayers. [43] Then fear came upon every soul, and many wonders and signs were done through the apostles. [44] Now all who believed were together, and had all things in common, [45] and sold their possessions and goods, and divided them among all, as anyone had need. [46] So continuing daily with one accord in the temple, and breaking bread from house to house, they ate their food with

gladness and simplicity of heart, [47] praising God and
having favor with all the people. And the Lord added
to the church daily those who were being saved."
Here is God's corporate testimony coming into existence as the church for the first time.

The outpoured Spirit was embodied in three
thousand people, and the evidence was the willingness of the Head in the members — willingness to
sell their houses and their possessions and to give
unselfishly to everyone. How could you get people
to do that? It was not legislated. It was not a rule in
the church in Jerusalem that to become a member of
the church you had to give up your bank account, you
had to give up your property. But when the Spirit was
poured out, the believers touched the willingness of
the life that opens its hand to all the members in a
spontaneous way. The atmosphere was open. Everyone simply poured out what they possessed. It
was an atmosphere of freedom, of giving, because it
was springing from the life of Christ Himself embodied in the church. The church was being made known
and God was being made known through the practical living of the saints, in their willingness to serve
one another and care for one another in practical

ways. This was the testimony in the church life.

Then Acts 4:32-33 says, [32] "Now the multitude of those who believed were of one heart and one soul; neither did anyone say that any of the things he possessed was his own, but they had all things in common. [33a] And with great power the apostles gave witness to the resurrection of the Lord Jesus." This was the testimony that Jesus was alive. The resurrection was more than a doctrine. Here the believers were connected with the transmission of such a Person, and it was being expressed in this kind of willingness. Then verses 34-35 continue, [34] "Nor was there anyone among them who lacked; for all who were possessors of lands or houses sold them, and brought the proceeds of the things that were sold, [35] and laid them at the apostles' feet; and they distributed to each as anyone had need." How do you explain this? Look at the tabernacle. Look at the temple. Look at the recovered temple. Now look at the church. What is the one factor that ties them all together? The people offered willingly. The saints gave willingly. This all shows that the genuine nature of the church life is in willingness springing up.

The first issue in the church life over willingness

The first negative incident in the church life involved an abuse of the willingness. Acts 5:1-4 says, [1] "But a certain man named Ananias, with Sapphira his wife, sold a possession. [2] And he kept back part of the proceeds, his wife also being aware of it, and brought a certain part and laid it at the apostles' feet. [3] But Peter said, Ananias, why has Satan filled your heart to lie to the Holy Spirit and keep back part of the price of the land for yourself? [4a] While it remained, was it not your own? And after it was sold, was it not in your own control?" This means that the church is not a place where anyone is forced. Do not be a hypocrite here. Do not play church. Do not feel that you have to do something in an outward way. That is not the nature of God in the church. Notice, Peter had to say, "Don't you know this was your own?" Then he continues in verse 4, "Why have you conceived this thing in your heart? You have not lied to men but to God." This means that this couple made a mere outward show of giving to the Lord, since it was without the proper heart.

Peter's response to their hypocrisy shows strongly

that the church must preserve an atmosphere in which every saint is genuinely — out of willingness — giving themselves to the Lord. If I give my money, if I give my time, if I spend my life, if I move for the church, if my job does not control me but the vision of the church controls me — if I give myself in that way — do not interpret this in an outward way, that "this is what we do here." We are not in that realm. Brothers and sisters, we are touching a life that is so mighty and so consuming for God's house that it is willing to pour out everything for that.

Everyone's integrity must always be preserved in the church life. There should be no coercing, no compelling, and no forcing, but only an atmosphere of freedom so that willingness can spring up. Do not ruin this atmosphere by commanding, by coercing, by putting people under a sense of obligation. That is too low. That is not the vision of the tabernacle, the temple, the recovered temple, and the early church. Indeed, all the saints were pouring themselves out because the giving God was living in them and was pouring out. Oh, saints, this is a vision. The Lord is speaking to us in this way.

THE SOURCE OF WILLINGNESS

Willingness is Christ

To experience Christ is to touch the willingness of this Person who has zeal for His Father's house and is building that house and must be about His Father's business (John 2:17; Matt. 16:18). Christ is of this nature. So whenever willingness surfaces within your heart — willingness calibrated to the church, God's house, God's dwelling place — you have met Christ in your mind, emotion, and will. You meet Him as the disposition of willingness surfacing within you. The evidence that He is taking you over and possessing your heart is that feeling in you of willingness to lay down your life for the saints and for His house. When willingness springs up, you have met Christ. The Lord Jesus is a Person and He feels like willingness. This is how you know you are touching the real Person and not a mere doctrinal concept or belief — you find God's disposition springing up within you. Our highest privilege and dignity is to participate in this willingness which is Christ Himself.

Willingness is in the new covenant

Now that we have seen Christ as the source of willingness, let us see willingness in the new covenant. The Mediator of the new covenant says, "I will put My laws in their mind and write them on their hearts" (Heb. 8:10). This is the way He works with us. He works with the grain of our being, not against the grain. For us to live the church life requires willingness, because there are no official committees and there is no official service. There is nothing official. What happens is that willingness springs up within us and we simply group together and pour ourselves out in a spontaneous way to meet the needs. This is because Christ in us is this way.

Christ writes His disposition into us. We must understand that willingness for the Lord, willingness for His interest, is not in you and is not in me. This should relieve us. It should relieve the pressure that comes with being in a false position and taking condemnation because you feel unwillingness in you. Of course you are not willing. No one is naturally willing for the church life. That is why Paul prayed such a strong prayer that we would be strengthened into our inner man, that Christ could make home in our heart, that we could be rooted and grounded in love. Then we could apprehend the knowledge-surpassing love of Christ with all saints (Eph. 3:14-21). This is an impossible life to live. But God has imparted that life into our spirit. And now this willingness is being written into our disposition. He is writing His very nature and life into our mind and into our heart. So willingness is in the new covenant as we enjoy and participate in our Christ.

Willingness is the life in our spirit

Romans 8:10 says, "If Christ is in you . . . the spirit is life." And in Matthew 26:41 the Lord says, "The spirit indeed is willing." The Lord knew that if He could exercise the spirit while under the pressure of His soul in Gethsemane, if He could pray and pray again, by touching His spirit He would find that willingness. Because He found that willingness, He went all the way to the cross. And now that very willingness, which is His life, is in our spirit.

Willingness is the nature of the life in our spirit. That is why we do not need to be discouraged when we see how unwilling we are. We are not even willing to take out the trash. We see our unwillingness. It catches us by surprise. For example, a need may arise, and we find we are not that willing to meet the need. But we have a spirit, and the life in our spirit is willing. So we can simply cut across our unwillingness and say, "Amen, Lord. Thank You for being my life." Then we find ourselves giving in because we have a spirit that gives in. Thank God for this willingness in our spirit.

Willingness in consecration is filling our hand with Christ

Now let us see how willingness is directly related to filling our hand with Christ. First Chronicles 28:21 says, "Here are the divisions of the priests and the Levites for all the service of the house of God; and every willing craftsman will be with you for all manner of workmanship, for every kind of service; also the leaders and all the people will be completely at your command." Notice it does not say "every craftsman" but "every willing craftsman." Then 1 Chronicles 29:5 says, "the gold for things of gold and the silver for things of silver, and for all kinds of work to be done by the hands of craftsmen. Who then is willing to consecrate himself this day to the LORD?"

Here again we see the word "willing." We may think consecration means "Now I am going to work something up." But in Hebrew, consecration simply means "filling the hand." In the Old Testament it was the priests who filled their hands with offerings. So consecration is to fill your hand with Christ.

The burnt offering, more than any other offering, shows the absolute willingness of Christ. He was absolutely consumed for the Father's good pleasure. He fulfilled the Old Testament type of the burnt offering — the offering that was placed on the altar, wholly consumed, and became a sweet savor to God for His good pleasure. So fill your hand with Christ as the Burnt Offering.

What is consecration? It is to recognize that I am not the one who is absolute and willing. I am not for God. My flesh is totally not for God and will never be for God, but I can lay my hand upon Christ. I can say, "Lord, thank You that You are the Burnt Offering. You are the willing One. And thank You for transmitting into me that willingness. This is the day of Your power. Because You are interceding as our Melchizedek, there is a willingness springing up on this earth."

There are saints whose hearts are stirred for the church, who want to live for it, who want to work for it, who want to move for it, who want to see the church spread on this whole earth. This willingness is not a result of being coerced or of being challenged, but of participating in the Burnt Offering. Who is living all the way to the end for God's good pleasure? It cannot happen in you and it cannot happen in me. It will never happen in any of us, regardless of how much natural energy we have. All of our natural effort will fizzle out. There is only one way to live fully for God's good pleasure. It is by the transmission of the Burnt Offering into our being. By this transmission there is a genuine experience of willingness.

Again 1 Chronicles 29:5 says, "Who then is willing to consecrate himself this day to the LORD?" Who is willing to fill his hand with Christ? Who is willing to keep touching Him, calling "Jesus!" When you see unwillingness surface in you, what should you do? Don't say, "Oh, look, I am not willing." Say, "I will never be willing. This is the way I am always going to be. In the flesh I am always going to feel that unwillingness." We are all the same. It is not that some are naturally more consecrated. No. The most consecrated person knows he is the most wretched person in himself. But he knows how to lay his hand on the Burnt Offering. This is how willingness happens. It happens by this transmission.

First Chronicles 29:6 says, "Then the leaders of the fathers' houses, leaders of the tribes of Israel, the captains of thousands and of hundreds, with the officers over the king's work, offered willingly." And verses 9-10 say, [9] "Then the people rejoiced, for they had offered willingly, because with a perfect heart they had offered willingly to the LORD; and King David also rejoiced greatly. [10a] Therefore David blessed the LORD before all the assembly." Here David broke out into praise and prayer. Joy was there because of the willingness. Whenever there is joy and willingness among us, we have met Christ. He is making Himself known. He is making Himself known in all the places on the earth — wherever there is a participation in this Person who is willingness. This is how willingness for God's house happens.

THE SIGNIFICANCE OF WILLINGNESS

Reward comes to serving with willingness

We see the significance of willingness in 1 Corinthians 9:16-17. Paul says, [16] "For if I preach the gospel, I have nothing to boast of, for necessity is laid upon me; yes, woe is me if I do not preach the gospel! [17] For if I do this willingly, I have a reward; but if against my will, I have been entrusted with a stewardship." This means that in one way or another, the gospel is going to be preached. But Paul speaks of reward. This is related to the kingdom and entering into the joy of "your Lord" (Matt. 25:21, 23). We do not want to be a person who is serving begrudgingly — "I have to do this." Rather, we want to do it willingly, to have a reward. Reward comes to serving with willingness.

How do you serve in the church? How do you care for the practical needs? Do you say, "Well, this is what the church does, and because I am here I should do it too. The brothers talked about the need for so many things. I should help too." We may hear of needs and respond in this outward way. But, brothers and sisters, it is another thing to have a deep realization that none of us are worthy to pick up a shovel for the Lord's house. We need the cleansing of the blood to touch any aspect of the house of God, the church of the living God (1 Tim. 3:15). We are not worthy. So we say, "Lord, thank You that You have washed me. You have made me a priest. Thank

You that I can handle You and can have within me such a desire and a willingness for Your house."

Whatever we do unto the Lord, however small it is, will bring the kingdom reward one day. The Lord will say, "Well done, good and faithful servant." So this is the significance of willingness in our being — it brings reward. What is crucial is not how many talents you have — five, two, or one — but the willingness in using your portion.

Willingness within our capacity
determines the worth of our serving

Concerning giving, 2 Corinthians 8:12 says, "For if there is first a willing mind, it is accepted according to what one has, and not according to what he does not have." This verse speaks of willingness within our capacity. It is not what you do not have. It is what you do have. It is the time you do have. It is the money you do have. It is what we do with what we have. Some have a greater amount of time. Some have a greater amount of money. But we may be like the little widow with two mites. The Lord looked at her and said, "This poor widow has put in more than all; for all these out of their abundance have put in offerings for God, but she out of her poverty has put in all the livelihood that she had" (see Mark 12:41-44; Luke 21:1-4). Though the others gave more monetarily, in God's sight she gave more because her heart was in it, the willingness was in it. When the atmosphere is this way in the practical church life, there is a savor of Christ in whatever we do. This is how God is made known. He is made known in the willingness of His people.

Willingness testifies to our relationship with the Lord and with the Body

Willingness is like a barometer of our real state with the Lord and with the Body. In 2 Corinthians 8:3-5 Paul refers to the willingness of the churches of Macedonia: [3] "For I bear witness that according to their ability, yes, and beyond their ability, they were freely willing, [4] imploring us with much urgency that we would receive the gift and the fellowship of the ministering to the saints. [5] And this they did, not only as we had hoped, but first gave themselves to the Lord, and then to us by the will of God." Paul says that they freely, willingly, gave much. Their willingness was an indication that their relationship with the

Lord was fresh and their relationship to the Body was real and genuine.

This shows us that a lack of willingness, a closed life, a self-centered life, a tight-fisted life, indicates a deficiency in our relationship with the Lord and with the Body. Many times we have fellowshipped about some urgent need. I know in my spirit immediately whom to call to care for that need. Some saints are available at a moment's notice. They are just ready for anything, without hesitation, without calculating. I do not mean there are not legitimate circumstances that may prevent us from being able to meet a need. But the point is, are we willing? Do we have relationships with one another in this kind of way? Such willingness indicates the health of our relationship with the Lord and with the Body.

When you see your lack of willingness, what do you do? You say, "Wretched man that I am, but Lord, grow in me. Thank You for Your life in me. I lay my hand on You as the Burnt Offering. You are the willing One. So, Lord, keep transmitting." Saints, the more we pray day by day, the more we touch our Melchizedek. And this is the day of His power. So on this earth, more and more saints are becoming willing for the church life. It is happening before our very eyes. We just rejoice in this reality.

Willingness expresses God's care dwelling in us

In 2 Corinthians 8:16-17 we see that willingness expresses God's care dwelling in us. In verse 16 Paul says, "But thanks be to God who puts the same earnest care for you into the heart of Titus." The verb "puts" is in the present tense, so it could literally be translated "is putting." God is putting the earnest care into the heart of Titus. Titus embodies God's heart toward the Corinthians. Then Paul continues to speak of Titus in verse 17: "For he not only accepted the exhortation, but being more diligent, he went to you of his own accord." Titus was not just outwardly responding to an exhortation here. The phrase "of his own accord" means that he went to the Corinthians "willingly." This means that Titus' willingness was the outward expression of God putting care into his heart. How precious that the willingness which expresses God Himself is embodied in a brother.

Willingness with our money is a sign of life

In 1 Timothy 6:17-19 Paul warns those who are

rich. In effect he says, "If you are rich, you have to heed a warning: Be quick and ready to give. Be willing to fellowship, ready to dispense." In other words, Paul says that those who have more should be ready. Even the Greek words used here mean "ready to give and fellowship" and "willing to share." Then Paul adds, "that they may lay hold on eternal life." This means that the way to lay hold on eternal life is to touch that life that is willing to give. We know that the Lord touches us all in this area. This is the area that will touch our heart and deal with our heart. The willingness to pour out practically, financially, is a manifestation of the genuineness of our laying hold of eternal life. This is the significance of willingness.

WILLINGNESS IN THE CHURCH LIFE

Preserving willingness in personal relationships

Now let us look at willingness in the church life. Paul says in Philemon 14, "But without your mind I wanted to do nothing, that your good deed might not be by compulsion, as it were, but voluntary." The word "voluntary" can also be translated "willingly." Paul did not want to automatically take Onesimus,

Philemon's runaway slave, and keep him. He could have sent a letter to Philemon and asked, "Could I keep Onesimus here?" But he actually sent him back to Philemon with a letter, saying, "without your mind, I would do nothing." In other words, Paul did not want to behave toward Philemon in a way that would create an atmosphere in which Philemon would be compelled to send Onesimus to him. This is a small point, but it is a major factor in the church life, that is, we should always preserve willingness in our personal relationships with the saints. Here Paul was taking care of the freedom of the saints.

Even when Paul speaks about giving, he is careful. In 2 Corinthians 9:7 he says, "So let each one give as he purposes in his heart, not grudgingly or of necessity." The Greek words for "not grudgingly" are very expressive. They mean "not out of grief, not out of a let-down feeling" — "I have all this money, and I was going to keep it, but now someone has a need." Then Paul continues in verse 7, "for God loves a cheerful giver." "Cheerful" comes from the Greek word *hilaros,* which when transliterated is the English word "hilarious." God loves a hilarious giver. This shows how an abundance of willingness in our hearts overflows in giving.

In all the letters of the New Testament, Paul is always careful to preserve the atmosphere of freedom in the church. This is because if you destroy freedom, you destroy the whole realm in which willingness operates and in which the divine love can flow out. In the early church, after the day of Pentecost, even when the saints sold their land, it was not compulsory. They acted freely, out of the life of God. So we can see willingness expressed in the church life.

Preserving willingness between the co-workers

In relationship to James and Peter, Paul wanted the right hand of fellowship (Gal. 2:9). Fellowship could not be out of coercion. It could not be forced. It could not be legislated. Paul went to fellowship with these brothers, and they gave him the right hand of fellowship. This does not mean that they negotiated over every matter, checking with one another about their two separate spheres of work. But there was an atmosphere of willingness, at least between these brothers, and a mutuality of fellowship. They gave to Paul the right hand of fellowship, preserving the atmosphere of willingness.

The overcoming saints in the churches
are made up of the willing ones

Finally, the Lord comes to the churches in Revelation. He is burdened for overcoming saints. His word to all the churches is simply, "He who has an ear, let him hear what the Spirit says to the churches" (Rev. 2—3). Then in Revelation 3:20 He says, "Behold, I stand at the door and knock. If anyone hears My voice and opens the door, I will come in to him and dine with him, and he with Me." Then Revelation 22:17 says, "And the Spirit and the bride say, Come! And let him who hears say, Come! And let him who thirsts come. And whoever wills, let him take the water of life freely." These verses indicate that even at the very end of this age, when the Lord wants to come back, the principle of willingness remains the same.

The Lord will never get a testimony out of a coerced, forced, compelled environment. It must be out of willingness — "whoever hears the Spirit" and "let him hear what the Spirit says." Oh, brothers and sisters, may we let this be the controlling atmosphere wherever we go on this earth for the Lord's testimony. May our prayer be, "Lord, we want to touch

You as the Burnt Offering, as the willing One, and let You transmit that same life and nature into us." Then spontaneously the church life will spread on this earth — by the springing up of a life that is willing to pour itself out for God's building. Amen!

5 ▶ Measured and Escorted to Christ

The principle of being measured

Seeing the church, feeling the church, having a church-life disposition and willingness are all practically worked out in our experience by our being measured and escorted to Christ. So we need to see in the Bible the divine principle of measurement that governs God's relationship with man. God works with fallen man on the basis of this principle. First, He measures man according to His standard. Then this divine measurement becomes a demand upon man. This demand, in turn, reveals man's shortness and failure. Finally, man's realization of his failure is intended by God to escort him to Christ. In other words, the measurement and the subsequent demand of God is for one thing — to lead us to Christ to experience Another life.

God desires to be man's life-supply. The way He fulfills this desire is by first measuring man to expose his shortness; second, by this measuring He escorts man out of his own resources into God Himself as his boundless supply. In God's economy the measuring

Word of God is always intended to produce a standard beyond man's ability and capacity. Indeed, God's Word with its divine measurement and high demand, which far exceeds man's natural capacity, is the same Word that escorts man to God Himself over and over again. We see this principle governing God's relationship with fallen man, both in the Old Testament under the law and in the New Testament under the higher demand of the law revealed in the Sermon on the Mount (Matt. 5—7). Thus, we can say that *man's extremity* becomes *God's opportunity*.

The demand of the law

The demand of the law pushes man beyond his capacity. It exhausts him of his resources. When the law makes its demand upon the flesh, the flesh cannot do it. This failure results in a sense of discouragement within fallen man. He is discouraged because of his inability to measure up to the law of God. Of course, according to the principle of measurement, this is precisely what God intends to produce in man. Indeed, that weak feeling of inability and our discouragement over it become God's way of escorting us to Another life!

This principle is addressed by the apostle Paul in Galatians 3:21-24: [21] "Is then the law against the promises of God? Absolutely not! For if a law had been given which was able to give life, righteousness would have indeed been of law. [22] But the Scripture has shut up all under sin in order that the promise out of faith in Jesus Christ might be given to those who believe. [23] But before faith came we were guarded under law, being shut up unto the faith which was to be revealed. [24] So then the law has become our child-conductor [Gk: escort, or guide] unto Christ that we might be justified out of faith." We can see from these verses that the law has become our escort unto Christ. The law could not *give* life, but it did *lead* and *escort* us to life.

In Romans 7 the apostle Paul is a prime example of a person in whom this principle was operating. He was struggling with the demand of the law expressed in the tenth commandment, "You shall not covet" (v. 7). Unlike the other nine commandments that are related to actions, this particular commandment is a commandment on reactions. Basically, the Ten Commandments are commandments on actions, for example, "You shall not kill," "You shall not commit adultery," and "You shall not steal." These are commandments against certain actions. But God so designed the Ten Commandments that they would also include a commandment on reactions. In other words, no one escapes being short when measured by the high demand of God's Word.

The tenth commandment is "You shall not covet," or "You shall not feel that way," or "You shall not react the way you are reacting." It is a commandment on reactions. The tenth commandment shows how deep sin is in our being. Sin is not just in our actions; it is in our reactions. God's law exposes sin to the core of our nature, not merely on the surface of our being. Our very reactions are wrong and come short of the divine measurement. We are void of the divine love in our reactions. Thus, our fleshly reactions show us that we are sinful at a deeper level than our outward actions.

With the apostle Paul in Romans 7, the tenth commandment was a demand upon his inner being. What he did not want to do, even what he hated, is what he found himself doing. This chapter reveals the frustration of a man trying to be right, but continuously falling back into the sinful habits and patterns that he was in bondage to. The law as the divine standard and measurement did its work upon

Paul — it exposed his inability and weakness.

When we come to the end of Romans 7, we find a man who has been defeated again and again. He is defeated to the point of utter frustration, discouragement, and wretchedness. He cries out in verse 24, "Wretched man that I am! Who will deliver me from the body of this death?" Thus, the law did a perfect work over Paul — it escorted him to Another life. It guided him out of himself to Christ. It so measured him that he no longer was looking at himself or expecting anything from himself. He was absolutely turned to Another source — Another life. In verse 25 Paul breaks out and says, "Thanks be to God, through Jesus Christ our Lord!" This is an expression of a man who has been escorted to Christ.

However, many times when believers are being measured by the Lord, instead of being escorted to Christ, they are left in discouragement and depression. They are left with hopeless feelings, feelings of not making it and wanting to give up. Thus, it is imperative to see that the demand of the law is the principle that governs God's dealings with man. This demand is designed by God to produce certain effects in man — feelings of failure and frustration. It is these very feelings that serve to escort us to

Christ. God uses our frustration to lead us to Another source and life, that we might learn to become a partaker of Christ, our life.

The demand of the Lord's sayings

The Lord not only measures us by the law, but even more, He measures us by what He taught in Matthew 5—7. The Lord's sayings in this section of the Word reveal a higher demand than the Old Testament law. In Matthew 5:17-20 the Lord says, [17] "Do not think that I have come to abolish the law or the prophets; I have not come to abolish, but to fulfill. [18] For truly I say to you, Until heaven and earth pass away, one iota or one serif shall by no means pass away from the law until all come to pass. [19] Therefore whoever annuls one of the least of these commandments, and teaches men so, shall be called the least in the kingdom of the heavens; but whoever practices and teaches them, he shall be called great in the kingdom of the heavens. [20] For I say to you that unless your righteousness surpasses that of the scribes and Pharisees, you shall by no means enter into the kingdom of the heavens."

When the Lord speaks of having a surpassing

righteousness for entering into the kingdom, He is applying a finer measurement with a much higher demand than the law. The standard of the law could be compared to measuring in inches, but the Lord's sayings in Matthew 5—7 could be compared to measuring in picas, which are a small fraction of an inch. This means the measurement is much finer and more detailed.

The Lord's word in Matthew 5—7 measures our emotions, our attitudes, our reactions, our exaggerations, our comments about others — He measures it all! He measures our heart, He measures what we think, He measures the fantasies in our mind, He measures how we look at others, He measures lust, He measures anxiety. He measures how we react in situations that touch our selfishness and personal convenience, for example, going two miles instead of one, or giving our outward coat as well as our inner garment. Nothing escapes being measured.

If we were discouraged by the law of Moses, we are even more discouraged by Matthew 5—7. Indeed, the Lord reaches the point of saying in Matthew 5:48, "You therefore shall be perfect as your heavenly Father is perfect." To be perfect in this verse is to fulfill the demand to love exactly as the

Father loves. It is not merely putting up with our enemies, but praying for them and blessing them. Such a measuring of our love finds us all short, but at the same time it escorts us to Christ as our life and life-supply. When we are escorted to Christ, we become *partakers* of His love. This is why the Lord begins Matthew 5—7 with "Blessed are the poor in spirit, for theirs is the kingdom of the heavens" (Matt. 5:3). When we are poor in spirit we realize that in ourselves we do not have the divine love toward our enemies. We realize we are nothing and we can do nothing. It is this sense of nothingness that escorts us to Christ. The Lord's high standard is intended to cause disappointment over ourselves, so that we would be drawn away from our own energy and strength to the energy and strength of Another life.

When the Lord said that He did not come to abolish the law or the prophets but to fulfill, He meant that *He Himself* would be the fulfillment of all that He taught and commanded. In other words, He was saying, "I am living the perfect life. I am overcoming sin, the flesh, the world, and the devil. I am bearing the penalty for sin. I am going to be raised from the dead, and I will become a life-giving

Spirit to enter into you and fulfill in you all that I have spoken. Everything is now embodied in Me! Now just learn how to draw from Me, drink of Me, feed upon Me, depend upon Me, and abide in Me. Let your need and sense of nothingness, which comes from being measured by the divine standard, escort you into all that I am!"

The demand of our environment

Being measured and confronted by the divine demands is always for the purpose of escorting us to Christ. God not only uses the law and the Sermon on the Mount to measure us, but He also uses our environment. Our environment makes demands upon us that cause us to sense our frailty and weakness. How we meet our environments, face them, and interact with them is used by God to escort us to Christ. Environments include your husband, your wife, your children, your money, your job — all persons, matters, and things in your daily life that affect you. In fact, environment, according to the biblical understanding, is simply *that which affects us*. A stormy relationship can affect us, money problems can affect us, taking a thought about a past mistake can affect us. Whatever may affect us—this is environment. Environment is like the law making a demand upon us that is beyond our capacity to handle. Just as the law escorts us to Christ, God intends that our environmental trials would also escort us to Christ. This means that we accept the "all things" of Romans 8:28 as being under God's sovereignty. Categorically, all things are working together for good, because under the mighty hand of God they escort us to Christ.

Environment, which is measured out by God, is always pushing us a little bit too far. We have environments that we cannot cope with in ourselves. We get discouraged, we get depressed, we turn inward upon ourselves, we sigh — "How can I go on?" or "I can't make it." Oh, brothers and sisters, that's right! That's exactly right! God intends that our environments push us beyond our limits.

This experience of being pushed beyond what we are able to do becomes our guide to escort us to Christ. This was Paul's experience in 2 Corinthians 1:8-10: [8] "For we do not want you to be ignorant, brothers, of our affliction which befell us in Asia, that we were excessively burdened, beyond our power, so that we despaired even of living. [9] Indeed we ourselves had the response of death in ourselves, that we should not base our confidence on ourselves but on God, who raises the dead; [10] who has delivered us out of so great a death, and will deliver us; in whom we have hoped that He will also yet deliver us." Here Paul allowed his "despair of living" to escort him to the God who raises the dead, knowing that He would deliver him. Thus, again and again, every kind of demand in our environment is actually a divine escort in disguise to lead us to Christ.

A further example of the Lord's speaking concerning what He intends to accomplish through environmental dealings is found in Deuteronomy 8:2-3: [2] "And you shall remember that the LORD your God led you all the way these forty years in the wilderness, to humble you and test you, to know what was in your heart, whether you would keep His commandments or not. [3] So He humbled you, allowed you to hunger, and fed you with manna which you did not know nor did your fathers know, that He might make you know that man shall not live by bread alone; but man lives by every word that proceeds from the mouth of the LORD."

When the Lord said, "to humble you and test you," He meant "to measure you." When He said, "to know what was in your heart," He meant that in their hearts, the children of Israel would discover murmuring and rebellion manifesting itself, and they would find themselves coming short of God's standard. In other words, all their negative reactions to their environment were allowed by God to escort them to live by every word that proceeds out of the mouth of God.

The fact that the Lord allowed them to hunger and then fed them with manna signifies that they were pushed beyond their capacity in order that they would be escorted to eat divine food. To not "live by bread alone" meant to not live by the natural life, but by every word that proceeds out of the mouth of the Lord. God was seeking to escort them in the wilderness to learn to live by Him as their source and supply. In the same way, God humbles us through environments that we just can't cope with. It is at those junctures that we need to quickly recognize our escort! The feelings of not being able to cope *are* the escort. Our escorts leading us to Christ come in the form of frustration, desperate feelings, and failure. We need to recognize these escorts and allow them to guide us to live by manna! That is, we allow them to guide us to live by Christ as our bread!

The law is beyond our capacity. The Lord's sayings in Matthew 5—7 are beyond our capacity. Our environments also push us beyond our capacity. All of these things are absolutely God's favor to us, because He is not leaving us to ourselves. He exhausts us. He allows us to be defeated and feel discouraged. But the problem is this—we do not see that discouragement is our escort to Christ! May the Lord open our eyes to see what is happening to us in the midst of our reactions, that we might seize our discouragement and let it escort us to Christ.

Have you had any escorts lately? Praise the Lord! There is great hope in our escorts. They turn defeat into hope. The most defeated can use their very defeat as an escort to Christ. Whatever the Lord may expose in our lives — our reasoning mind, our divided heart, our motives — causes us to feel undone, naked, and defeated before Him. We need to realize at that time that the Lord is simply escorting us to Himself. Paul indicates this in Hebrews 4:13: "And there is no creature that is not manifest before Him, but all things are naked and laid bare to the eyes of Him to whom we are to give our account." Following this verse in which we are exposed to the core of our being, Paul says in verse 16, "Let us therefore come forward with boldness to the throne of grace that we may receive mercy and find grace for timely help." This speaks of being escorted to Christ *at the very time* of being naked and laid bare. Thus, all the demands and all the defeats are our personal escorts to Christ.

The demand of the law, the demand of the Sermon on the Mount, and the demands of our environment are all arranged by God to lead us out of our own limited capacity and ability. God's intention is to bring us into Another life. He wants us to touch the life that has already made it into glory! Touch the life Who is the victory! Touch the life that now dwells in our spirit!

Now we need to know how to turn to Christ in the midst of our problems and defeats. That is, we need to know how to touch the realm of the spirit and how to partake of the One that we are being escorted to. Without this turn to Christ we will still languish in ourselves. But, brothers and sisters, there is an installation in us! It is the installation of the Triune God. The Father is in the Son, the Son flows as the Spirit, and the Spirit is joined to our spirit (John 14:10-11; 7:37-39; 1 Cor. 6:17). When we open our mouths and contact such a God, we open ourselves to all the riches of the Godhead as our supply.

There is nothing that is too hard for Christ. He has already been perfected for us and has become the source of our salvation (Heb. 5:9). So what should we do with our defeatedness, our sense of discouragement, our reactions that say, "I can't do that! I can't be that way! I can't love that way!" Simply allow all these to become escorts to lead us to Christ.

The demand of the church life

The demand of the church life is another kind of experience that God uses to escort us to a richer and deeper Christ. This demand comes with the revelation of the church that is according to the New Testament apostles. Once we see the church by revelation, we see how short we are in our ability to live the church life. The most basic point related to the demand of the church life is to love as Christ loves. The church life requires loving one another not only *with* Christ's love but *in* His love — loving as Christ loves, loving all the saints for the building up of His unique one Body. This requires the divine love, the kind of love that is beyond our capacity, the kind of love that we do not have in ourselves.

The kind of church life described in the New Testament requires a higher and deeper love than we have in our natural life. We are called to love sinners. We are called to love those who are unfinished, who are still in the process of being transformed. We are called to love weak and oftentimes failing saints. Divine love is Calvary love, the love demonstrated on the cross. It is love that flows out to despicable kinds of people — ugly people, hateful people, dirty people, rebellious people, deceived people. The love of God in Christ is all-embracing and full of forbearance and longsuffering.

To have the church life that is unveiled in the pages of the New Testament demands this kind of divine love. It is a church life that is beyond the reach of our natural man. In ourselves we do not have the capacity to love one another the way Christ loves us. But that's okay! When we see the demand of the church life with its measurement, it should produce a sinking feeling in our self-life. But that sinking feeling, if properly understood, is really an escort to guide us to Christ. While we are sinking in a feeling of despair over ourselves, we begin to confess our inability and emptiness by saying, "Lord, there is nothing in me that could live the church life with the disposition of the divine love toward all the saints. But I thank You, Lord, for Your life in my spirit that can strengthen me. By Your strengthening You can make home in my heart to love through me with Your love." This kind of sinking yet confessing prayer is an escort to Christ. When we are overwhelmed with the demand of the church life, we are put more and more into contact with Another life that can supply us with divine love. Thus, the demand escorts us to Christ. Amen!

In the book of Ezekiel we see the principle of measurement at work. The last chapters of this book, describing the details of the temple, are a portrayal in typology of the church life in the New Testament. For example, in Ezekiel 43:10-12 we read, [10] "Son of man, describe the temple to the house of Israel, that they may be ashamed of their iniquities; and let them measure the pattern. [11] And if they are ashamed of all that they have done, make known to them the design of the temple and its arrangement, its exits and its entrances, its entire design and all its ordinances, all its forms and all its laws. Write it down in their sight, so that they may keep its whole design and all its ordinances, and perform them. [12] This is the law of the temple: The whole area surrounding the

mountaintop shall be most holy. Behold, this is the
law of the temple." When Ezekiel had the vision of
the temple, he was to measure the pattern. This
means that everything related to the temple was
measured according to the divine plan with its divine
dimensions. That measurement exposed the state of the
children of Israel. If they would allow the measurement
to produce shame for their iniquities, then that kind
of response would escort them to God and deeper
into the details of His building for His satisfaction.

The measuring process is opened up to us in
Ezekiel 47:1, 3-5: [1] "Then he brought me back to the
door of the temple; and there was water, flowing
from under the threshold of the temple toward the
east, for the front of the temple faced east; the water
was flowing from under the right side of the temple,
south of the altar. . . . [3] Then, when the man went out
to the east with the line in his hand, he measured one
thousand cubits, and he brought me through the
waters; the water came up to my ankles. [4] Again he
measured one thousand and brought me through the
waters; the water came up to my knees. Again he
measured one thousand and brought me through; the
water came up to my waist. [5] Again he measured one
thousand, and it was a river that I could not cross; for

the water was too deep, water in which one must swim, a river that could not be crossed." Thus, Ezekiel had a wonderful, marvelous escort that brought him through the measuring process.

We are all being measured. Our mind is measured under certain environments. For example, when we consider the matter of giving to the Lord, we are being measured. Our reasoning comes in — "I can't give." This environment is for the purpose of being escorted through the waters and brought into another level of life. In other words, this escort is an escort into life-supply. This supply will take us in our experience into a deeper Christ, a Christ beyond what we can ask or think. Here in Ezekiel there is a measurement over the house, and the measurement is according to the divine standard. Ezekiel is measured and escorted through the waters into more life-supply for a purpose — that water could flow out of the temple, God's house.

In the New Testament we are measured by the demand of the church life revealed by the apostles. It is not the kind of church life found in present-day Christianity with its shallowness and outwardness. The kind of church life in the New Testament is not denominational. It has nothing to do with being a

Baptist, a Methodist, a member of a Free Church, a charismatic, and so forth. The church life revealed in the Bible is without division. All genuine believers are members one of another. All are organically related to each other by Christ, and Christ alone! And all are being built up with one another in love, experiencing the cross with one another and practically meeting together in the oneness of the Spirit.

In contrast, in today's divided church, the self-life is not touched that deeply. In fact, you can remain in many places in the professing Christian world and never really be measured by the Lord. It is not a church life that demands everything in your life. It does not push you beyond the limit of yourself. It is only a convenient, so-called church life that centers totally on meeting your need, rather than creating a need in you to be escorted to Another life.

The church that is according to man's thought does not escort you to Christ. But the revelation of the church in the divine thought pushes you beyond your capacity, with the goal of escorting you to Christ. For example, the measurement of the church in the book of Ephesians goes far beyond our limited concept of the church. The seeming impossibility of the kind of church life described in Ephesians is in itself an escort to Christ. To have such a church life requires a deeper and higher experience of Christ. That is why Paul prays two specific prayers for the believers in Ephesians. We need to see the church by revelation, and we need to feel the church by our hearts being full of Christ and His knowledge-sur-passing love. Then we experience forgiving one another, enduring, suffering long, keeping the one-ness of the Spirit in the bond of peace, not being blown about by the wind of teaching. We find ourselves going beyond what we could ask or think in relation to living a church life.

The church according to God's thought goes beyond the ability of our natural life and demands that we be escorted to Christ as our life. When we talk about the church and giving our whole being to the church life, we may feel we can't make it. We just don't have the disposition for it. Our coming up short produces a kind of discouragement. Again, we have to say that according to the divine principle of measurement, God uses this discouragement to es-cort us to Christ. The church, in God's thought, requires Another disposition that we do not have in ourselves. That is why we are escorted to Christ. Paul prays this way — that we would be strengthened into our inner man, that Christ would come in and possess us, and even make home and settle down in our heart. It is by being escorted to Christ that we will have the capacity for the church life.

Oftentimes, we have been left with our flat, demoralized feelings. The demand of the law was there, the demand of the Lord's sayings was present, the demand of our environment was upon us, and the demand of the church life was ever before us. All these things were like high demands, yet we did not realize the demands were our escorts to lead us to "the rock that is higher than I." Hear what the Psalmist declares to the Lord: "From the end of the earth I will cry to You, when my heart is over-whelmed; lead me to the rock that is higher than I" (Psa. 61:2). This illustrates the proper understanding of being measured and escorted to Christ.

The demand of the kingdom

The divine principle of demand and measure-ment, which governs God's relationship with man, extends to the realm of the kingdom. The demand of the kingdom life is indeed beyond man's ability, as we see from the Lord's conversation with the rich young ruler in the Gospels. In Matthew 19:16-17 we read, [16]"And behold, someone came to Him and said, Teacher, what good thing shall I do that I may have eternal life? [17] And He said to him, Why do you ask Me concerning what is good? There is only One who is good. But if you want to enter into life, keep the commandments." Then the Lord graciously presented the various commandments. To this the young man replied, [20] "All these things I have kept. What do I still lack?" In answer to this question the Lord took the tenth commandment and applied it to the young man's life: [21] "Jesus said to him, If you want to be perfect, go, sell your possessions and give to the poor, and you will have treasure in the heavens; and come, follow Me." We see the young man's response to this word in verse 22: "But the young man, hearing this word, went away sorrowing, for he had many possessions." This word should have escorted him to Another life, but instead he went away sorrowing.

The young man's reaction to the demand of the kingdom to sell all was typical of fallen man — he was covetous and therefore not willing to sell his possessions. In other words, he failed the test. The Lord measured him by the tenth commandment and he was found wanting. The Lord then said to His disciples in verses 23-24, [23] "Truly I say to you, Only with difficulty will a rich man enter into the kingdom of the heavens. [24] And again I say to you, it is easier for a camel to pass through the eye of a needle than for a rich man to enter into the kingdom of God." By these words the Lord revealed the high demand of the kingdom life in relationship to man's lust and desires.

Then we read how the disciples responded in verse 25: "And when the disciples heard this, they were greatly astonished and said, Who then can be saved?" Again, the Lord had pushed the demand of the kingdom to the utter limits. Who is willing to give up all their possessions for the sake of the kingdom? This demand produced a reaction of astonishment in the disciples. They imagined that it was impossible for anyone to be saved. Thus, the demand of the kingdom is stringent and absolute, altogether unachievable to the natural man. As we have seen, when God presents this kind of demand, it is His way of escorting man to Himself.

To the disciples' question, "Who can be saved?" the Lord replied in verse 26: "And looking upon them, Jesus said to them, With men this is impossible, but with God all things are possible." This word indicates that the sorrowing feelings of the young man over his lack of willingness should not have led him away from the Lord; rather they should have escorted him to the Lord. By being escorted to the Lord, he could draw from Him all the possibilities that are in His life. The young man had the right reaction to the demand of the kingdom — he felt sorrowful over his greediness and recognized that in himself he could not let go of his possessions. At that juncture he should have allowed his inadequate feelings to escort him to the God who makes all things possible.

To properly understand the Christian life we need to apprehend this divine principle that governs God's relationship with man — wherever there is demand from God, there is always supply waiting to meet that demand. We only need to be escorted to the source of the supply. Whether it is the demand of the law, the Sermon on the Mount, our environmental dealings, the church life, or the kingdom — all are to lead us to Christ to interact and fellowship with Him that we might partake of His victorious life.

May this word govern us the rest of our lives. May we realize again and again that our weaknesses are our escorts out of ourselves into Another life. So when our flesh reacts to the Lord's measurement, instead of staying in the reaction or fueling the reaction, we need to allow the reaction to bring us to Christ in a specific way. Various kinds of reactions — discouragements, defeats, temptations — are all our escorts to experience more of Christ.

Brothers, yes, your flesh is lustful. Your lustful feelings affect you in a negative way, but walk in the Spirit and you will turn those feelings into paths to Christ. None of us can change our flesh (John 3:6). It is irreparable and unchangeable. However, as redeemed children of God, while we are still in these mortal bodies God uses the flesh to lead us to Christ over and over again! Therefore, when we allow our greatest weakness to escort us to Christ, it will become the factor of our greatest supply of life.

This was the apostle Paul's experience in 2 Corinthians 12. He had a "thorn in the flesh" (v. 7). It was a chronic problem that caused him to feel weak. He asked the Lord three times to remove it, but the Lord did not remove it according to his prayer. The Lord instead answered him with "My grace is sufficient for you, for My power is perfected in weakness" (v. 9). When Paul realized that God was using this environment to put a demand upon his flesh that was beyond his natural strength, he completely changed his attitude toward his thorn in the flesh. In verses 9-10 he says, [9b] "Most gladly therefore I will rather boast in my weaknesses that the power of Christ might tabernacle over me. [10] Therefore I am well pleased in weaknesses, in insults, in necessities, in persecutions and distresses, on behalf of Christ; for when I am weak, then I am powerful." In other words, Paul was saying, "When I am weak, I allow my weakness to escort me to Christ! It is in my weakness that He tabernacles over me and I draw from Him. Instead of my weakness being a frustration to my experience of the Lord, it becomes a path to lead me to the One who supplies me continuously with His grace."

Paul learned this through the demands in his environment. So none of us should allow any environments to embitter us. Instead they should sweeten us because they bring us so much God. In all the demands, God is teaching us one lesson — "I don't want you to live by your own life anymore. I am simply driving you out of yourself into Myself that I can be your All in all!" Oh, brothers and sisters, there are hundreds of hallelujahs within us as we learn to appreciate that all the demands in our lives are one escort after another, lined up, to lead us continuously to the all-sufficient Christ!

The demand of the New Jerusalem

The final measurement in the Bible revealing all that God is and all that He wants is found in Revelation 21—22. This is the most thorough measurement with the most exacting demand. The measurement comes in the form of a vision of the holy city, New Jerusalem. Revelation 21:15-17 says, [15] "And he who spoke with me had a golden reed as a measure that he might measure the city and its gates and its wall. [16] And the city lies square, and its length is as great as the breadth. And he measured the city with the reed to a length of twelve thousand stadia; the length and the breadth and the height of it are equal. [17] And he measured its wall, a hundred and forty-four cubits, according to the measure of a man, that is, of an angel."

According to Matthew 22:30, in the realm of resurrection man becomes like the angels of God in heaven. Therefore, the measure of a man being that of an angel simply refers to a measurement in resurrection. This means that the entire city of the New Jerusalem is measured according to the standard and demand of resurrection life. It is measured with a golden reed, signifying the divine nature. Thus, the measurement of the city reveals the Triune God with all His chosen and redeemed people for eternity. The city is composed of God's people fully transformed and supplied with God in the Lamb flowing as the river of the water of life.

The New Jerusalem is the consummation of all God's measuring and escorting throughout all the ages. The revelation of the city unveils what God requires: it is golden; it has the glory of God; it is holy; it is separate; it is the bride, the Lamb's wife; it is constituted with God through and through. One glance at the holy city in spirit will cause us to realize that we all have come short of the glory of God. It will also serve to escort us to Him who is our eternal supply as the tree of life and the water of life (Rev. 22:1-2).

Eventually, with whatever measuring we experience — related to the law, the Sermon on the Mount, our environment, the church life, the kingdom, or the New Jerusalem — the demand should always lead us to a higher and richer experience of Christ. God does not want to bring us down to a level of ministry which pleases man and makes man feel comfortable, without any exposure or conviction. No! He wants His demands to remain beyond the reach of our natural life so that we would be driven out of ourselves into Him. The New Testament ministry of the Word should always maintain the divine principle of God's measurements and demands. When this is a reality among God's people, we will be escorted to Christ to abide in Him for His rich supply (John 15:5). By this we will find ourselves drawing from the unsearchable riches of Christ (Eph. 3:8). We will not only see the church by revelation, but we will feel the church in our hearts with the same feelings of the One who loves her and gave Himself up for her. Amen.

Scripture Index

New Testament